SPACE COLORING BOOK

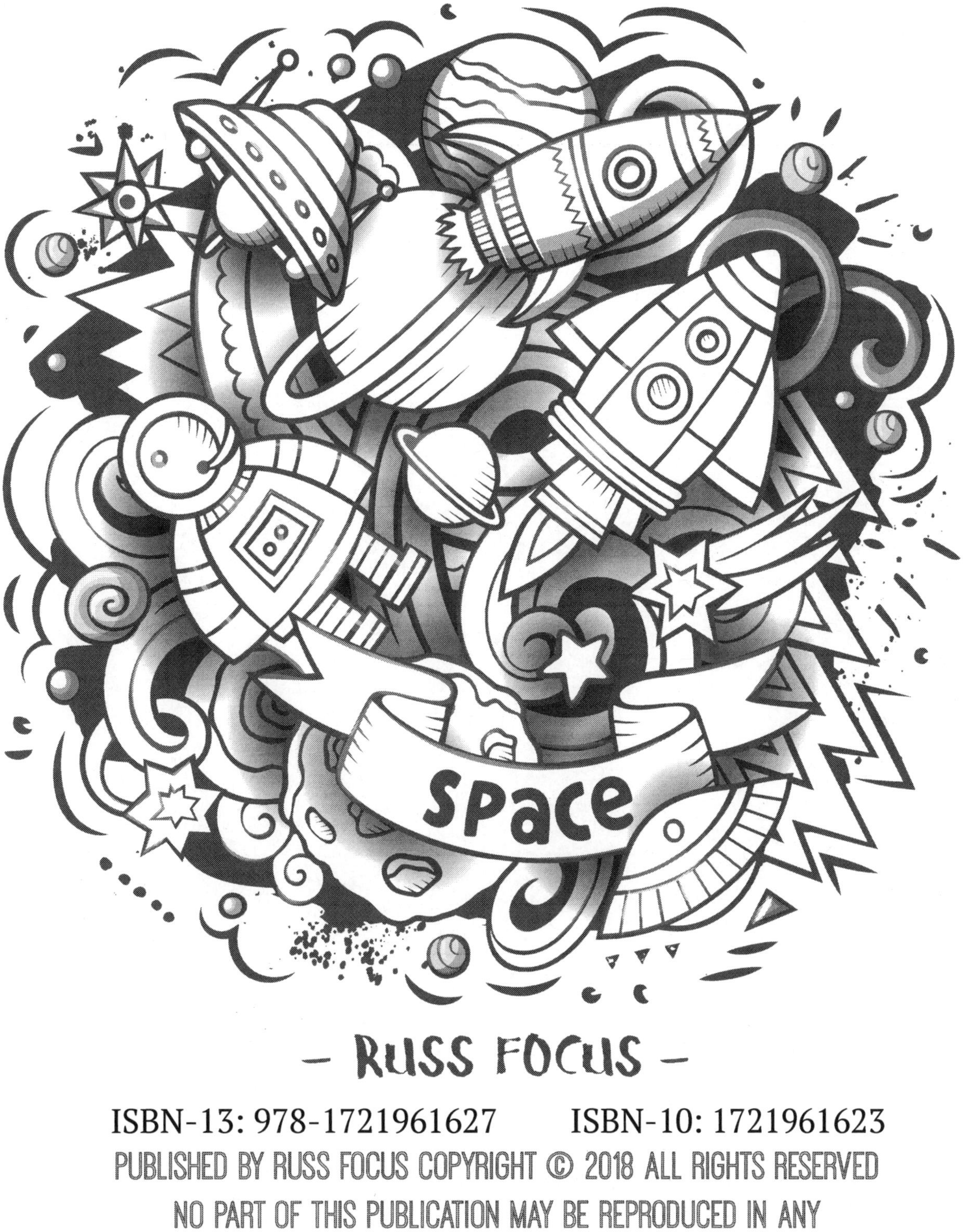

— RUSS FOCUS —

ISBN-13: 978-1721961627 ISBN-10: 1721961623

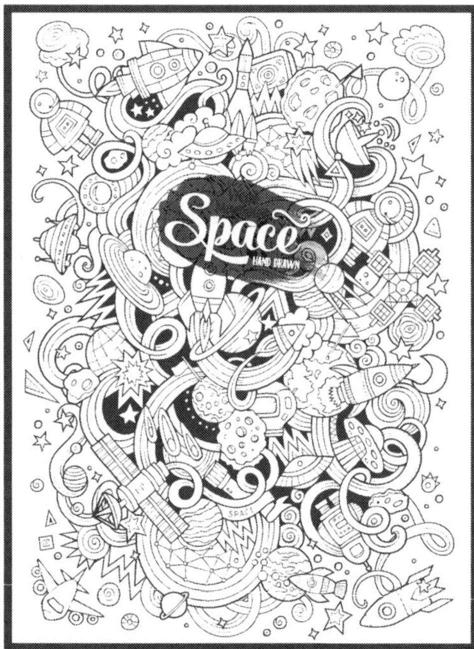

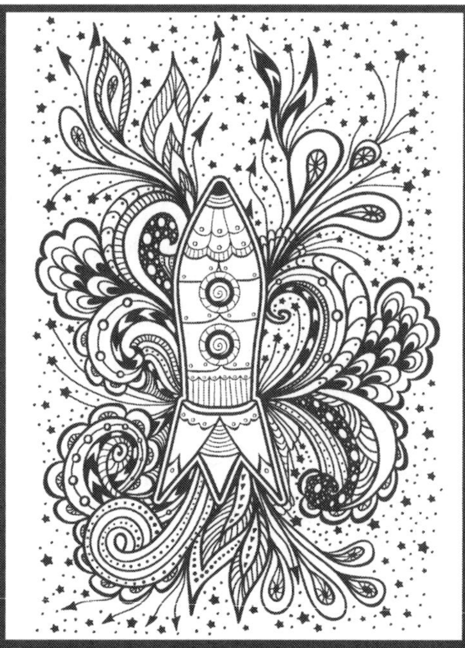

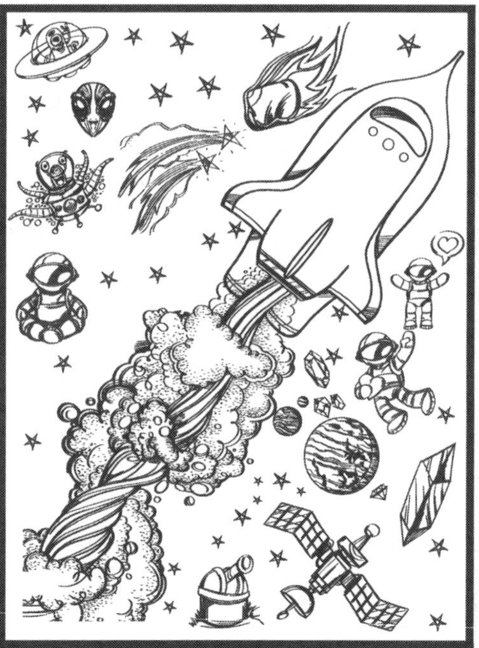

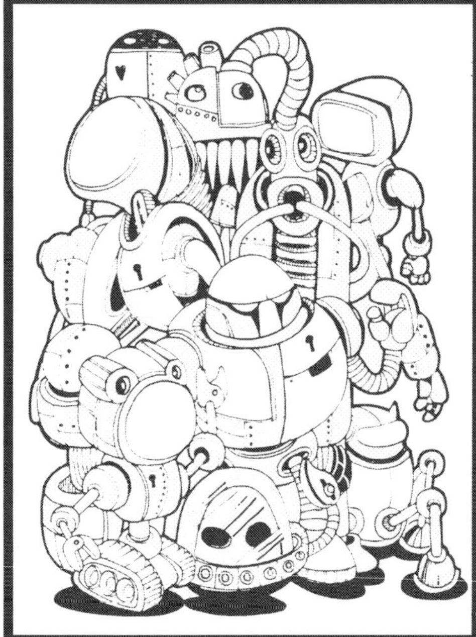

SAMPLE
SPACE
COLORING
17 of 42
PAGES

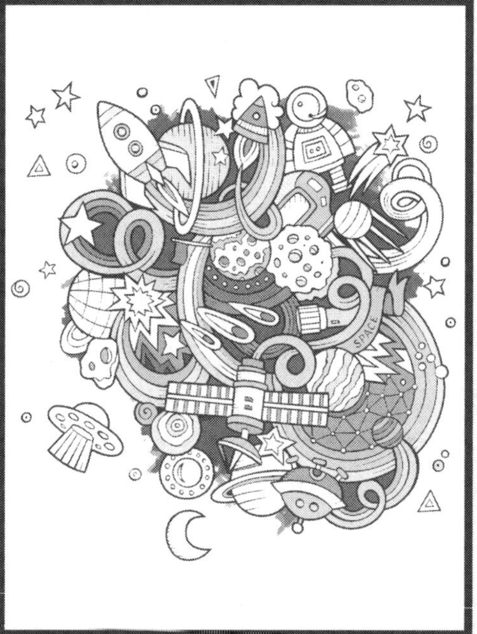

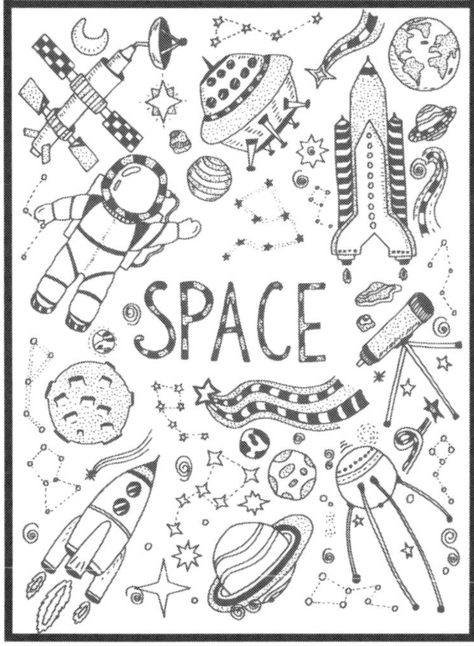

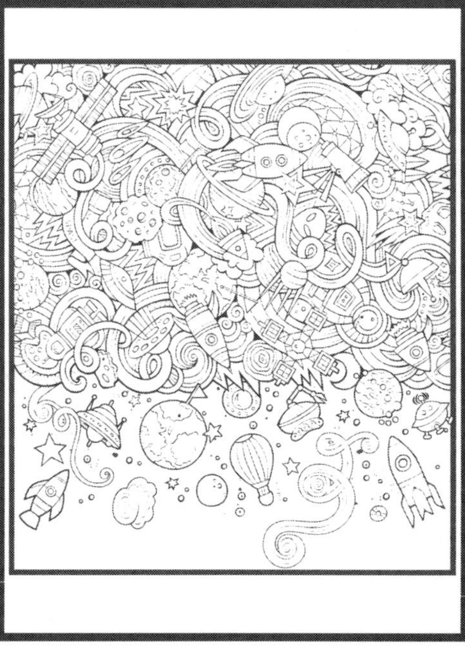

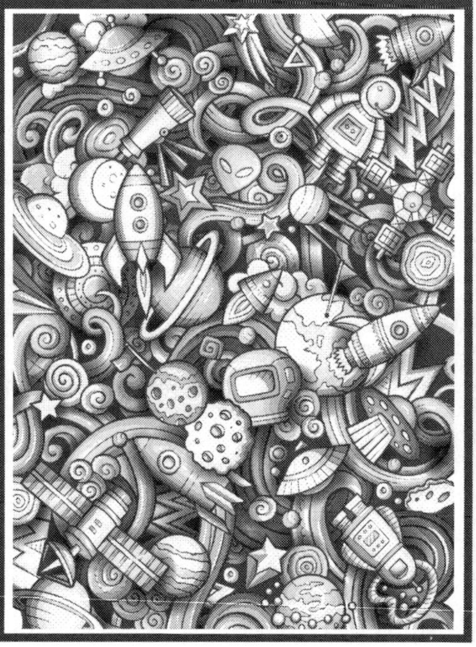

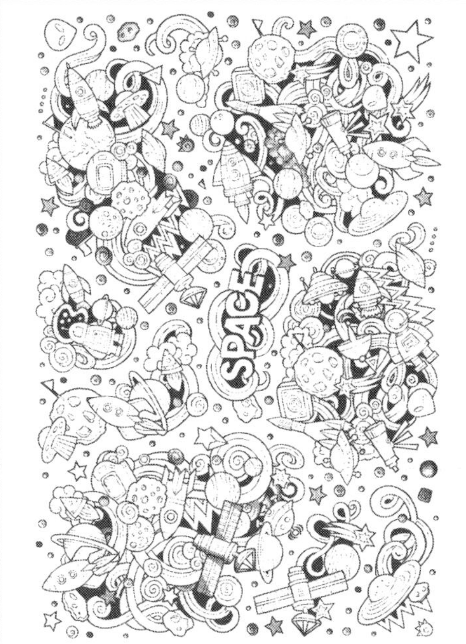
SPACE
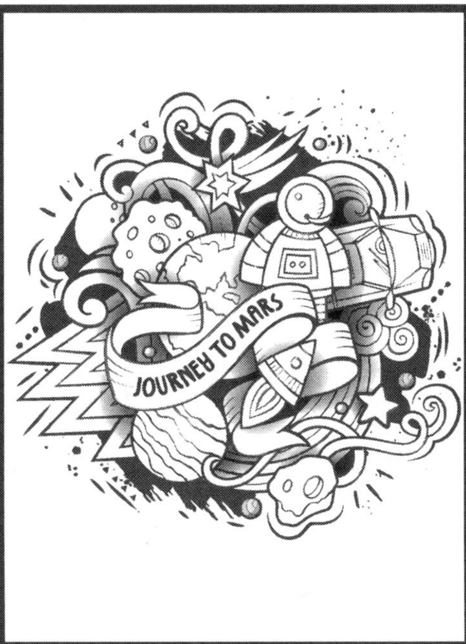
JOURNEY TO MARS
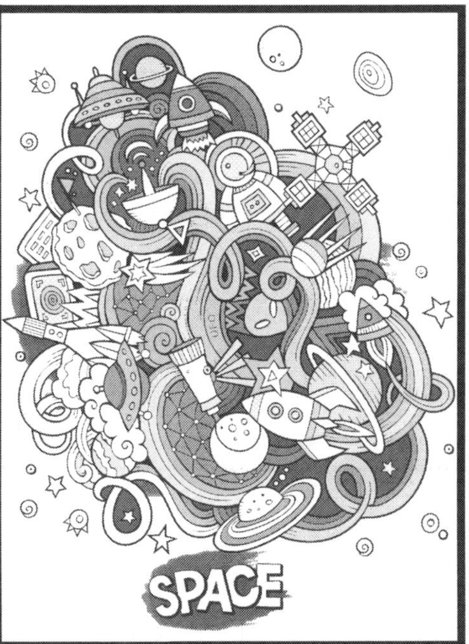
SPACE
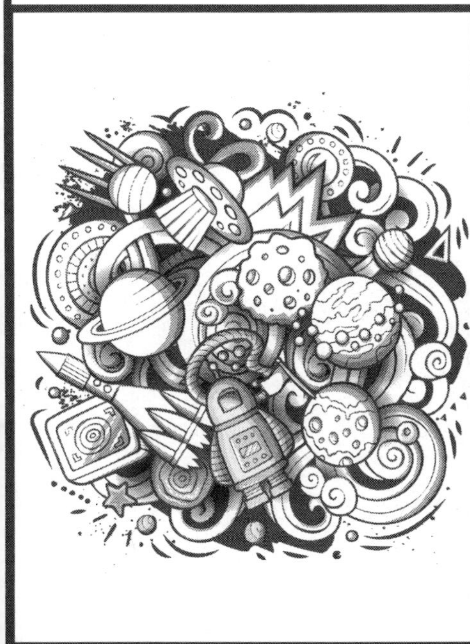
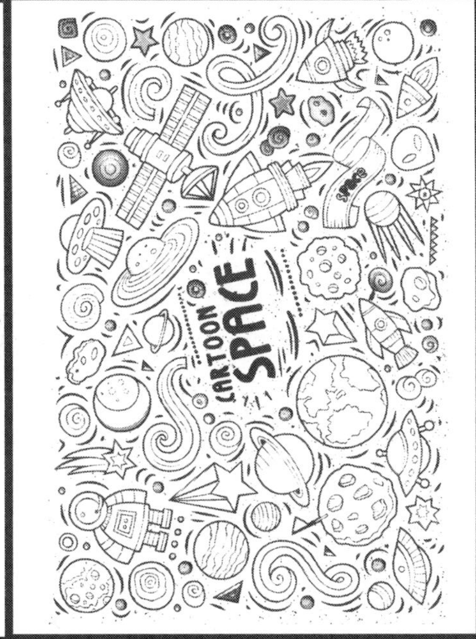
CARTOON
SPACE
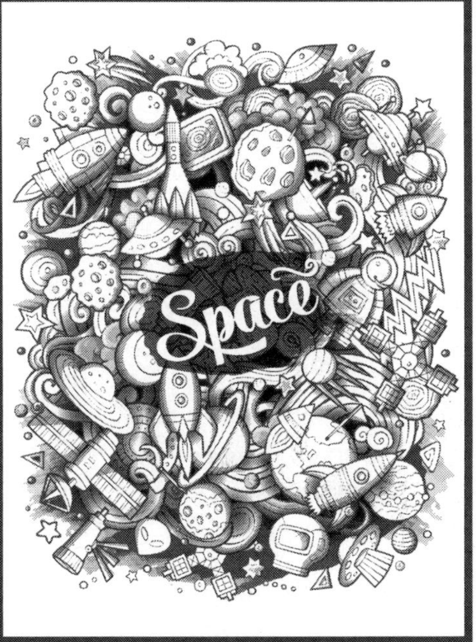
Space
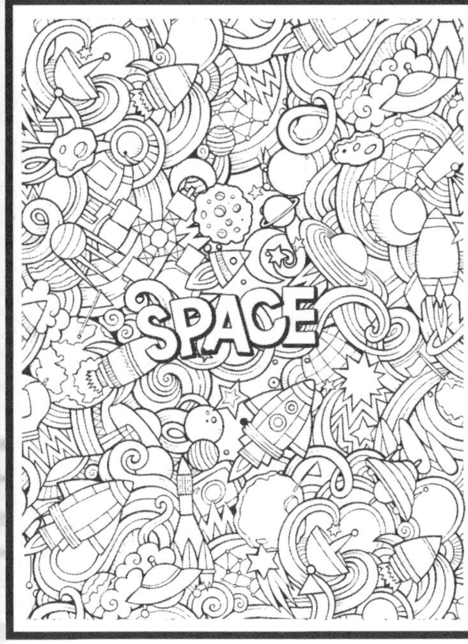
SPACE
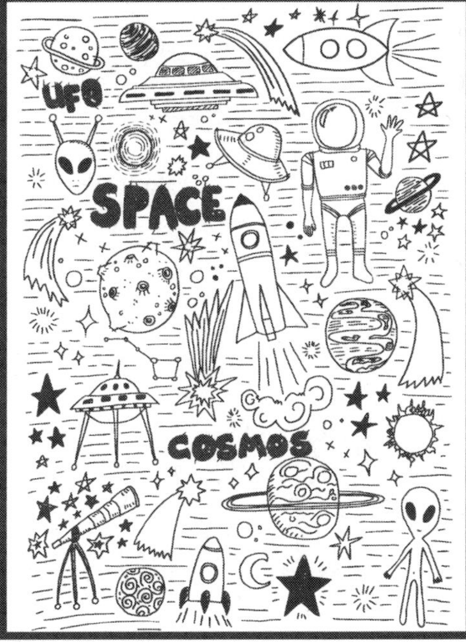
UFO
SPACE
COSMOS
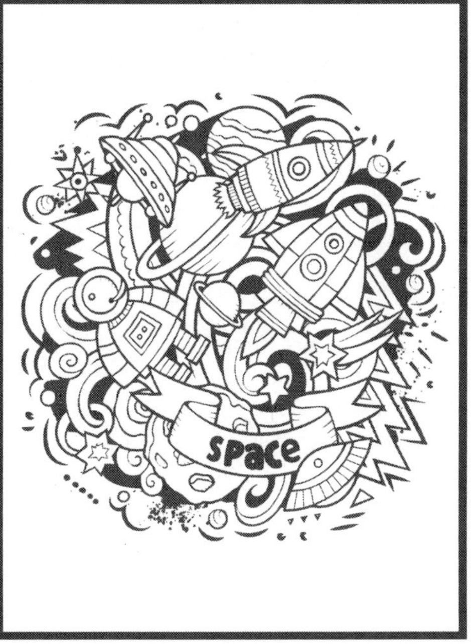
space

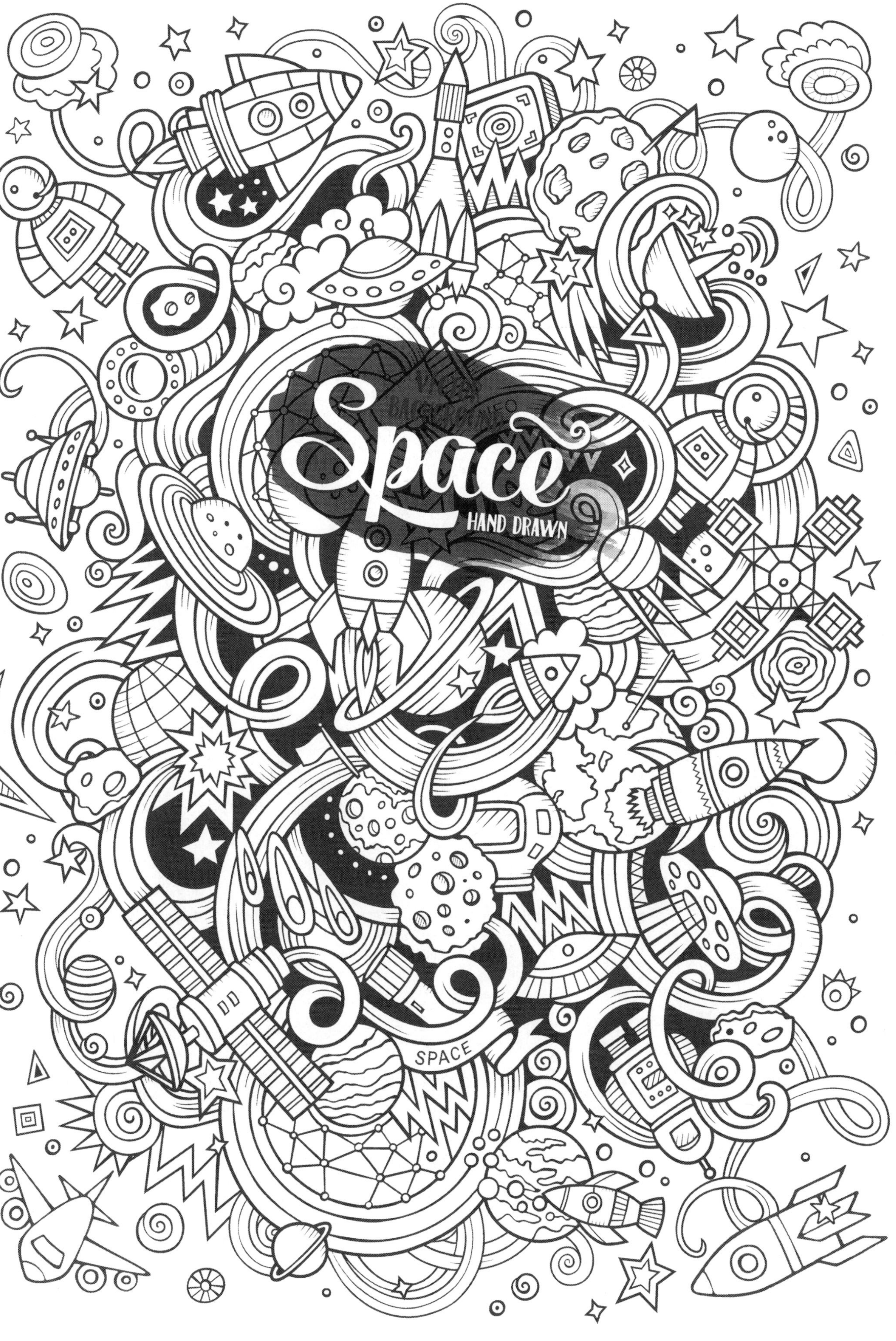
Space
HAND DRAWN
SPACE

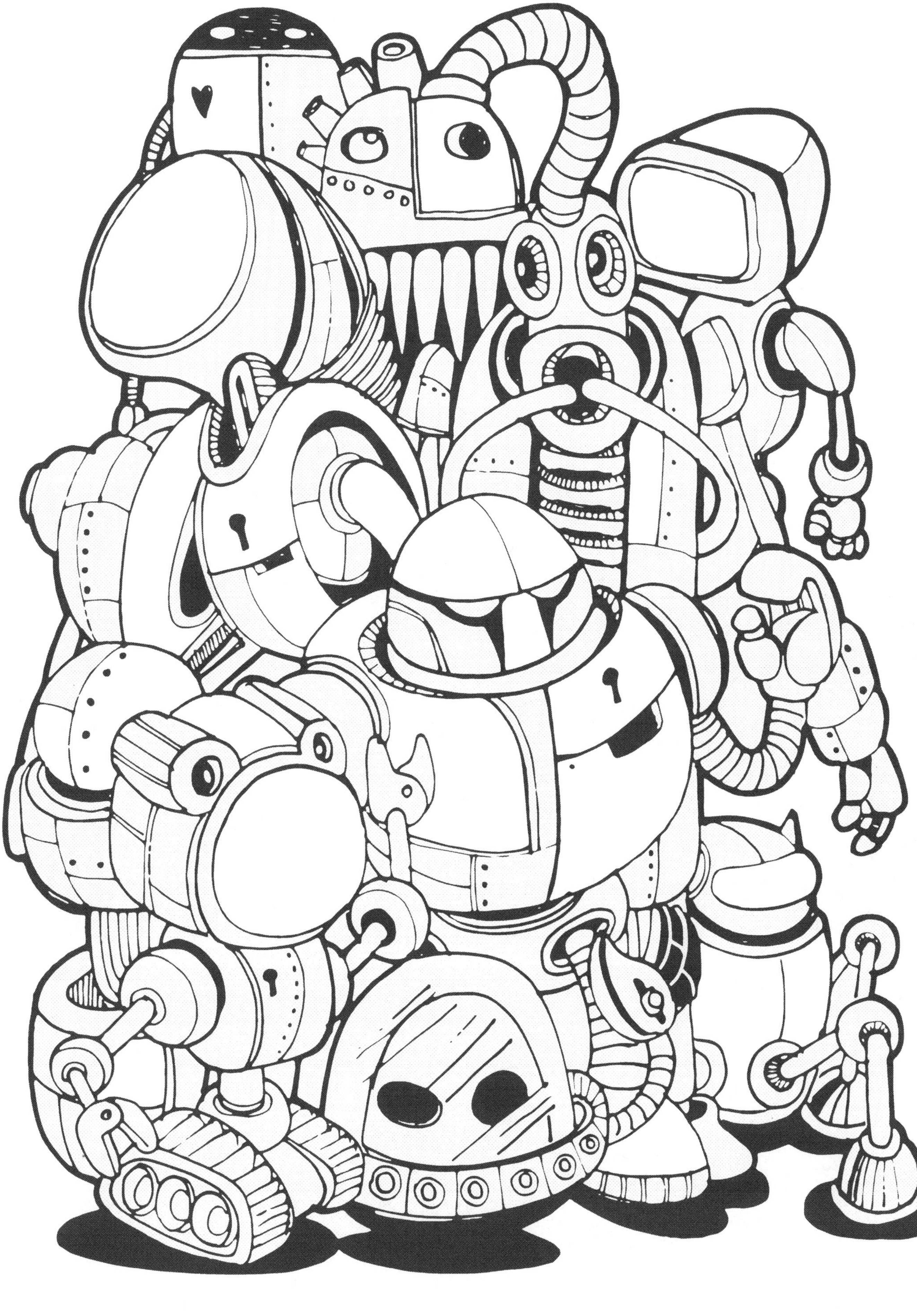

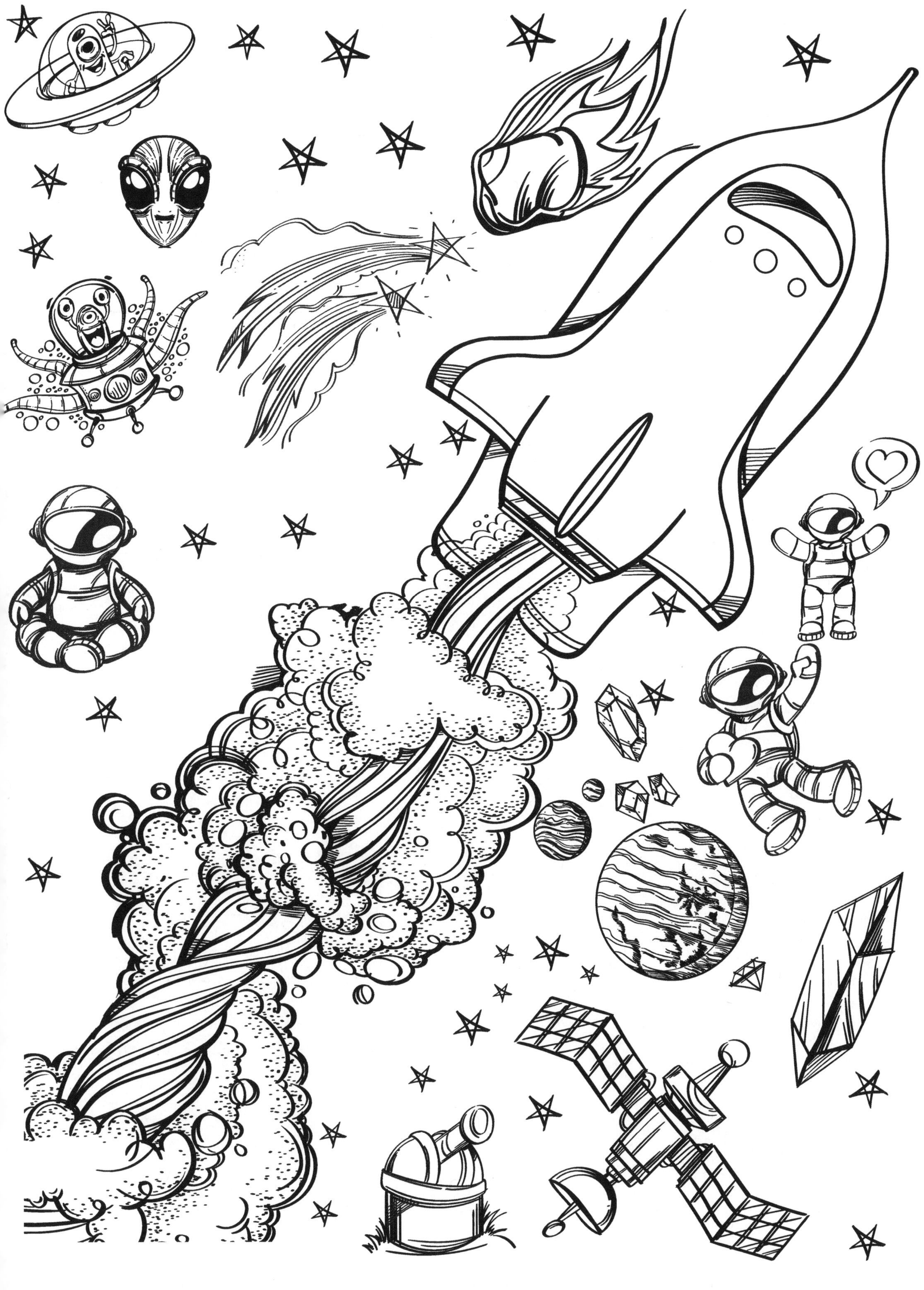

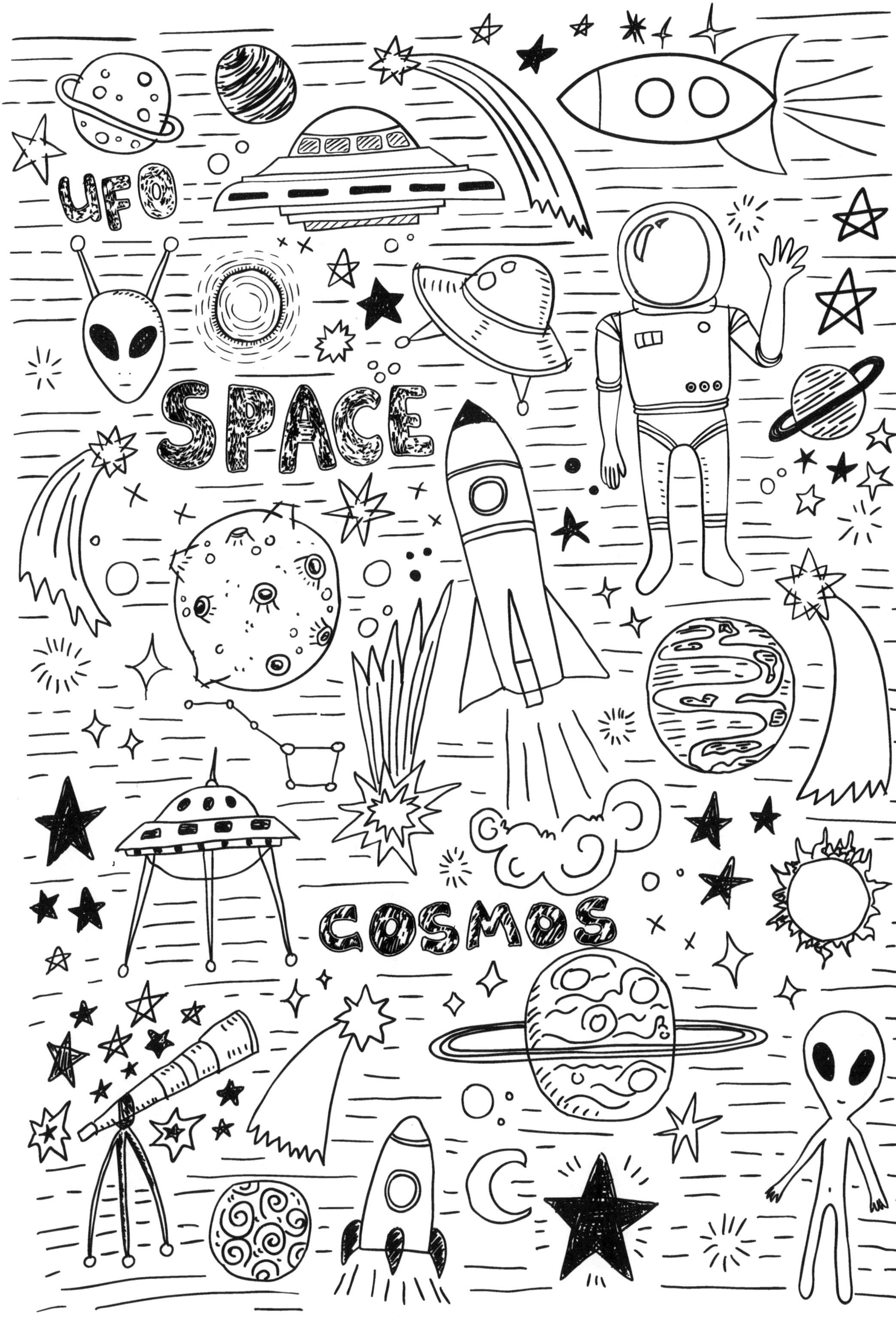
UFO
SPACE
COSMOS

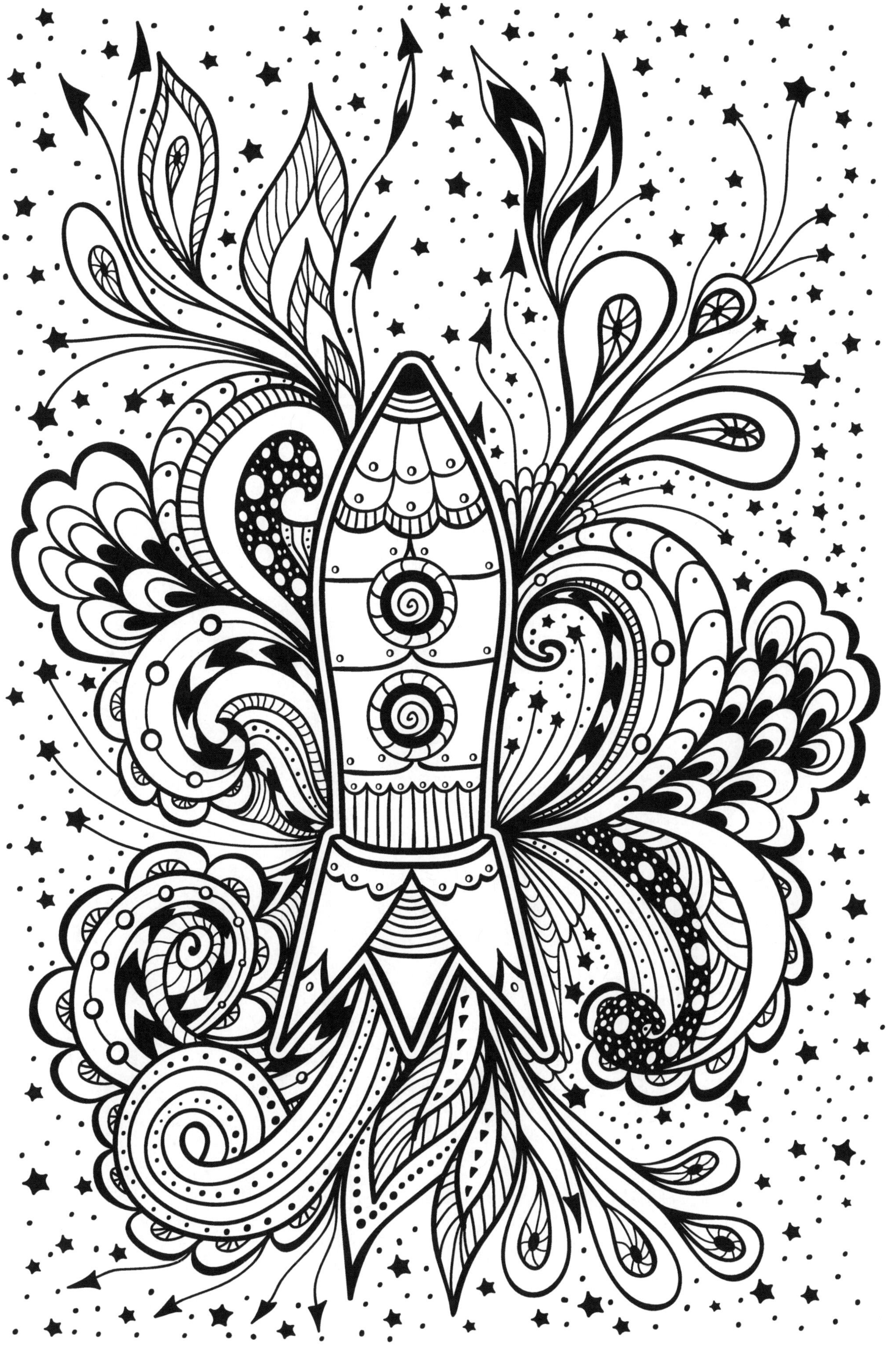

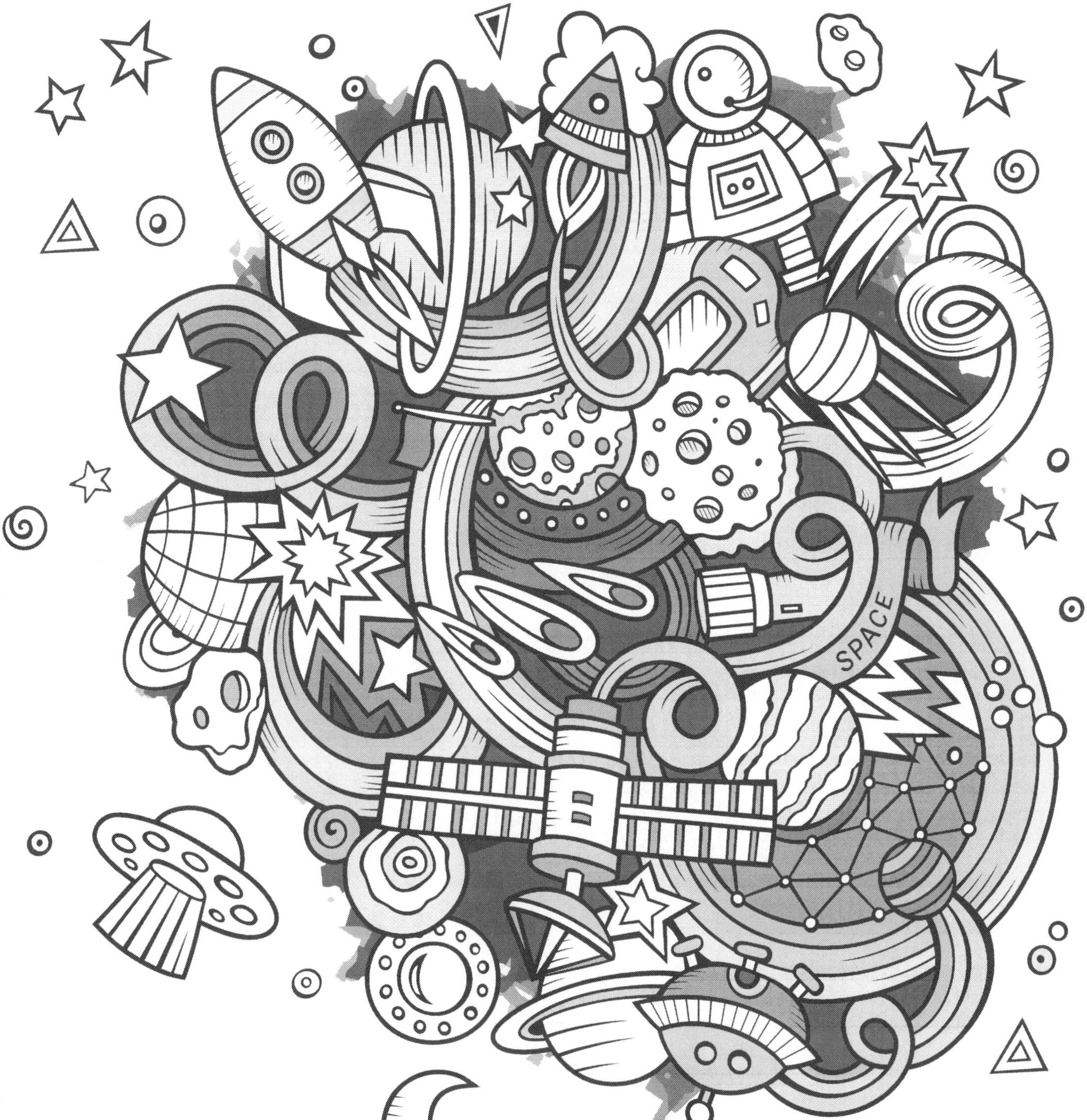
SPACE

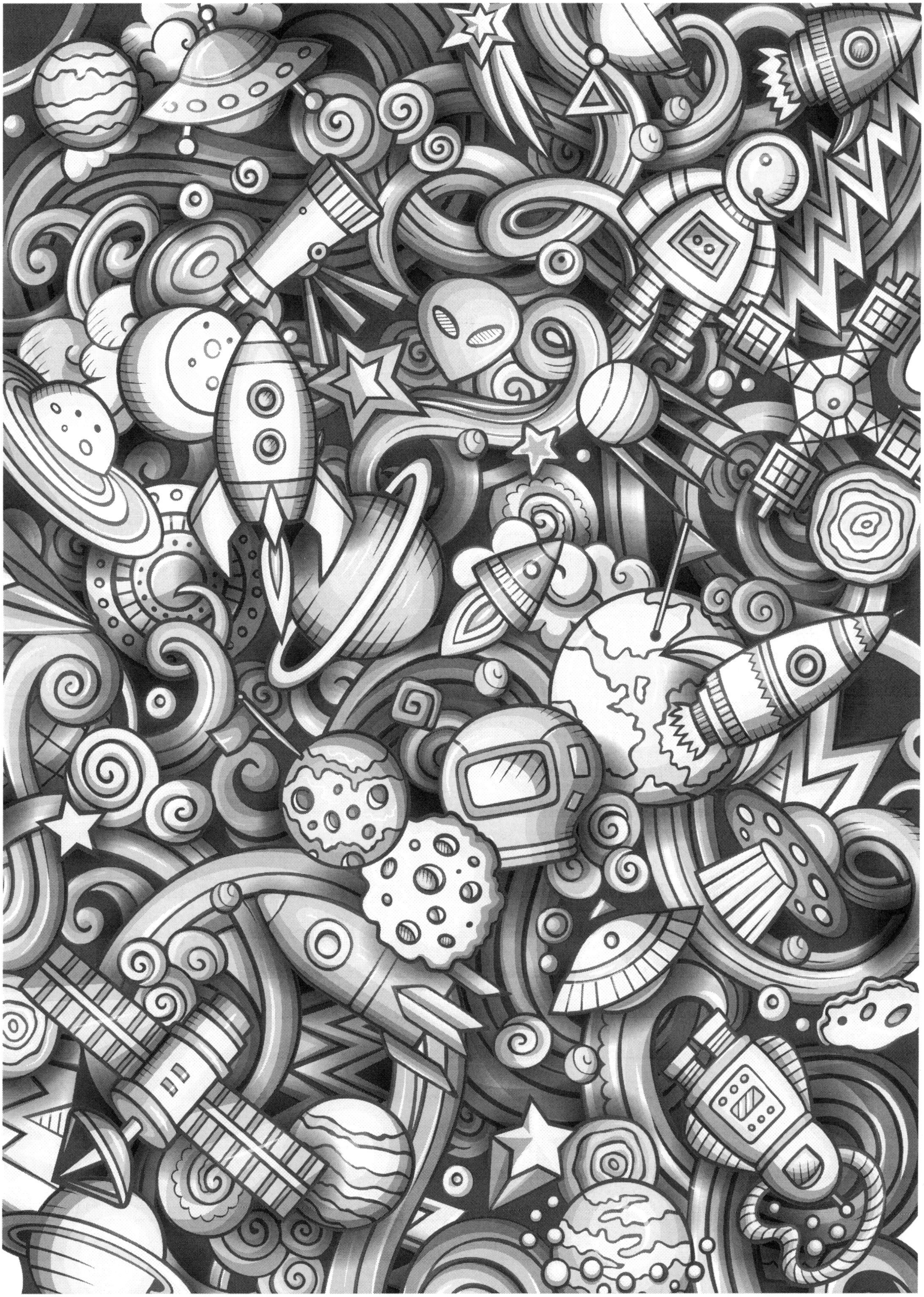

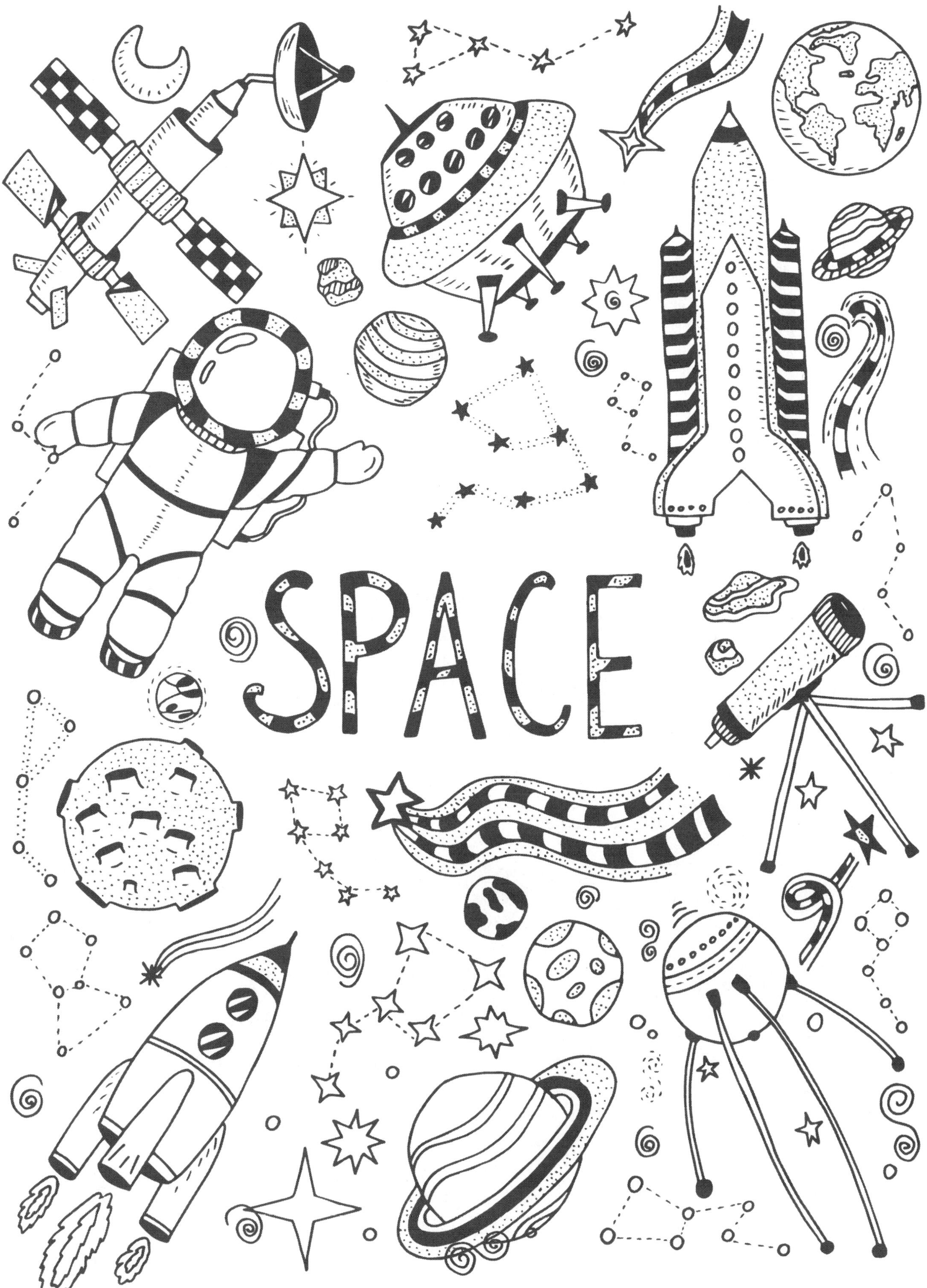
SPACE

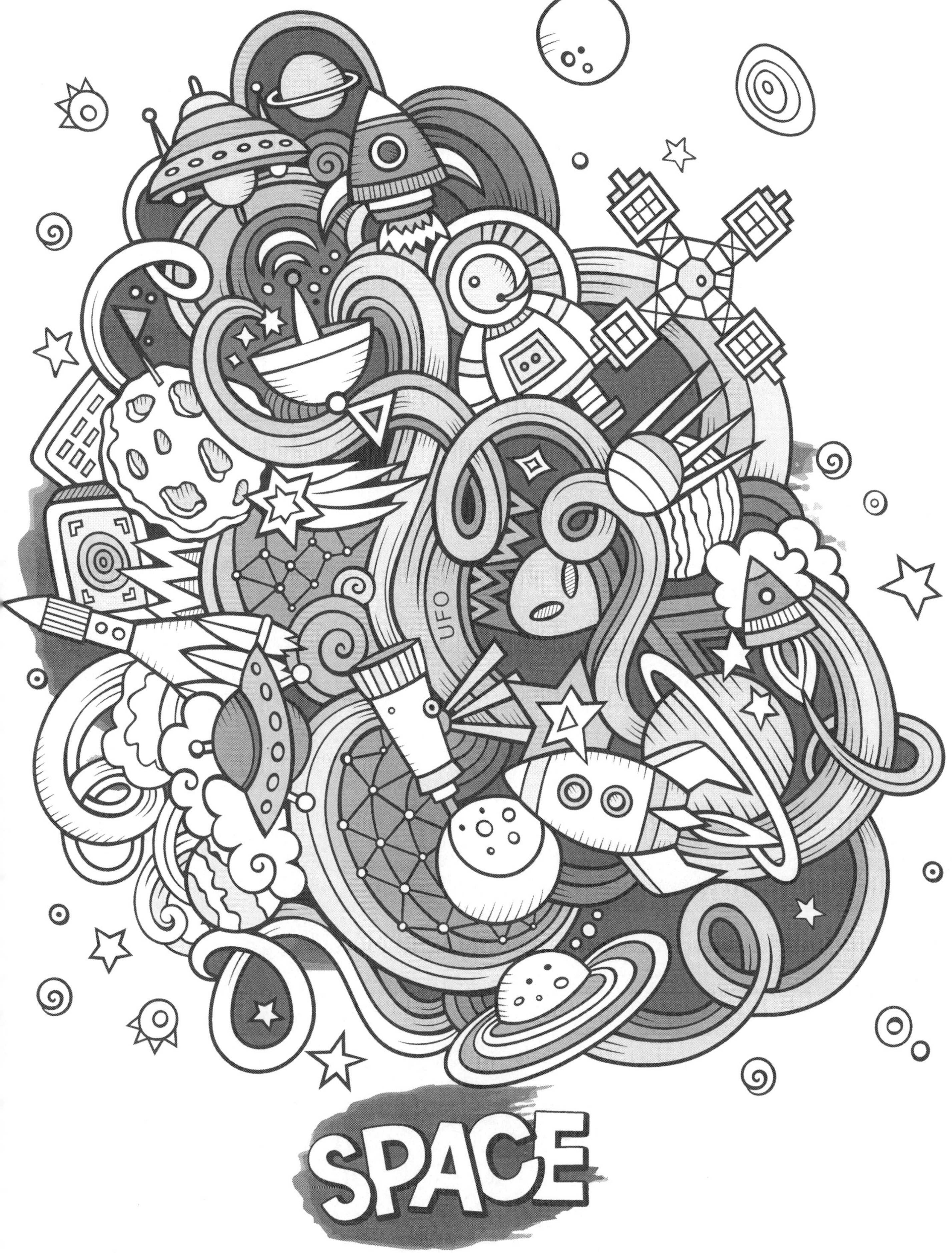

SPACE

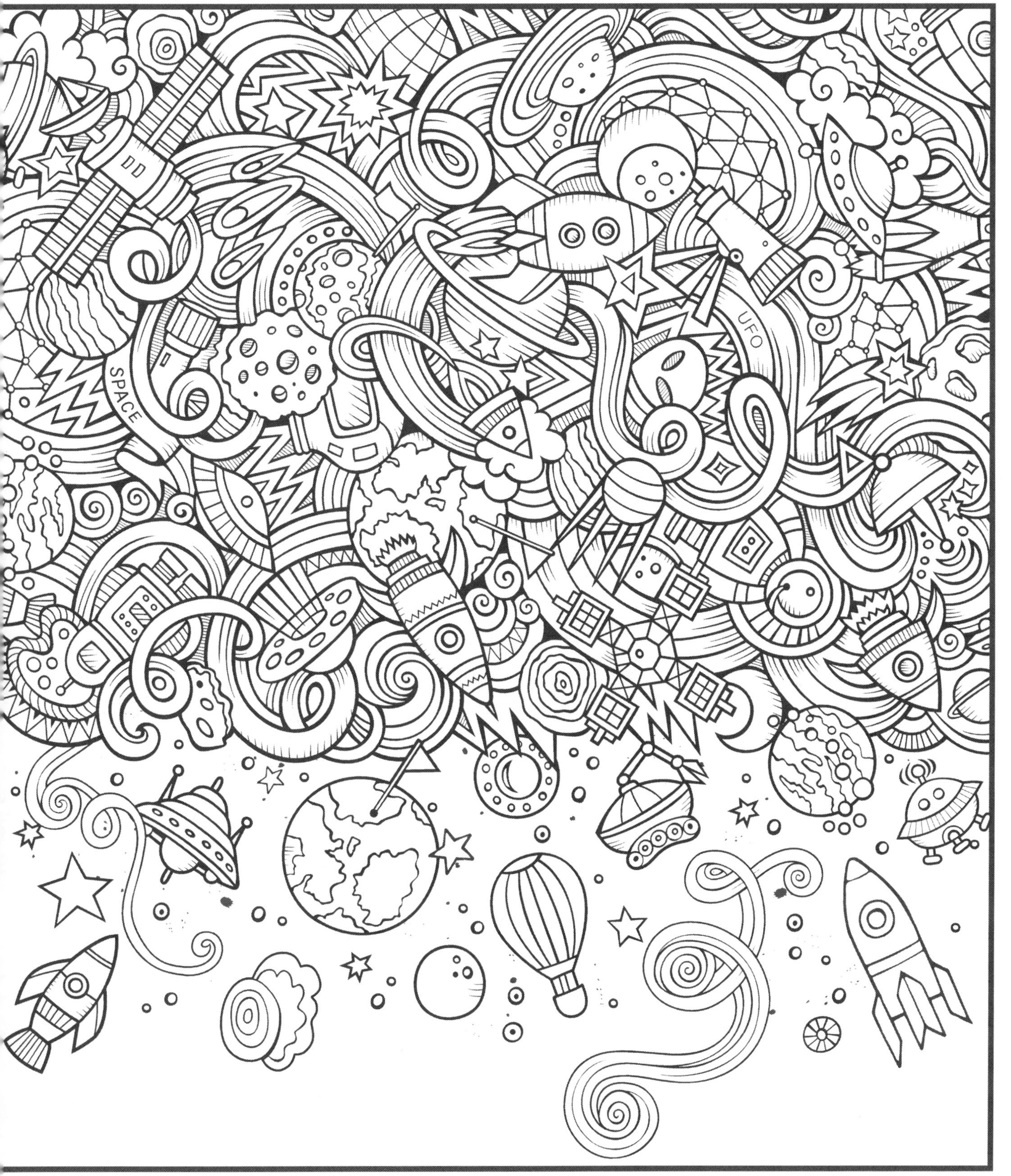
SPACE
UFO

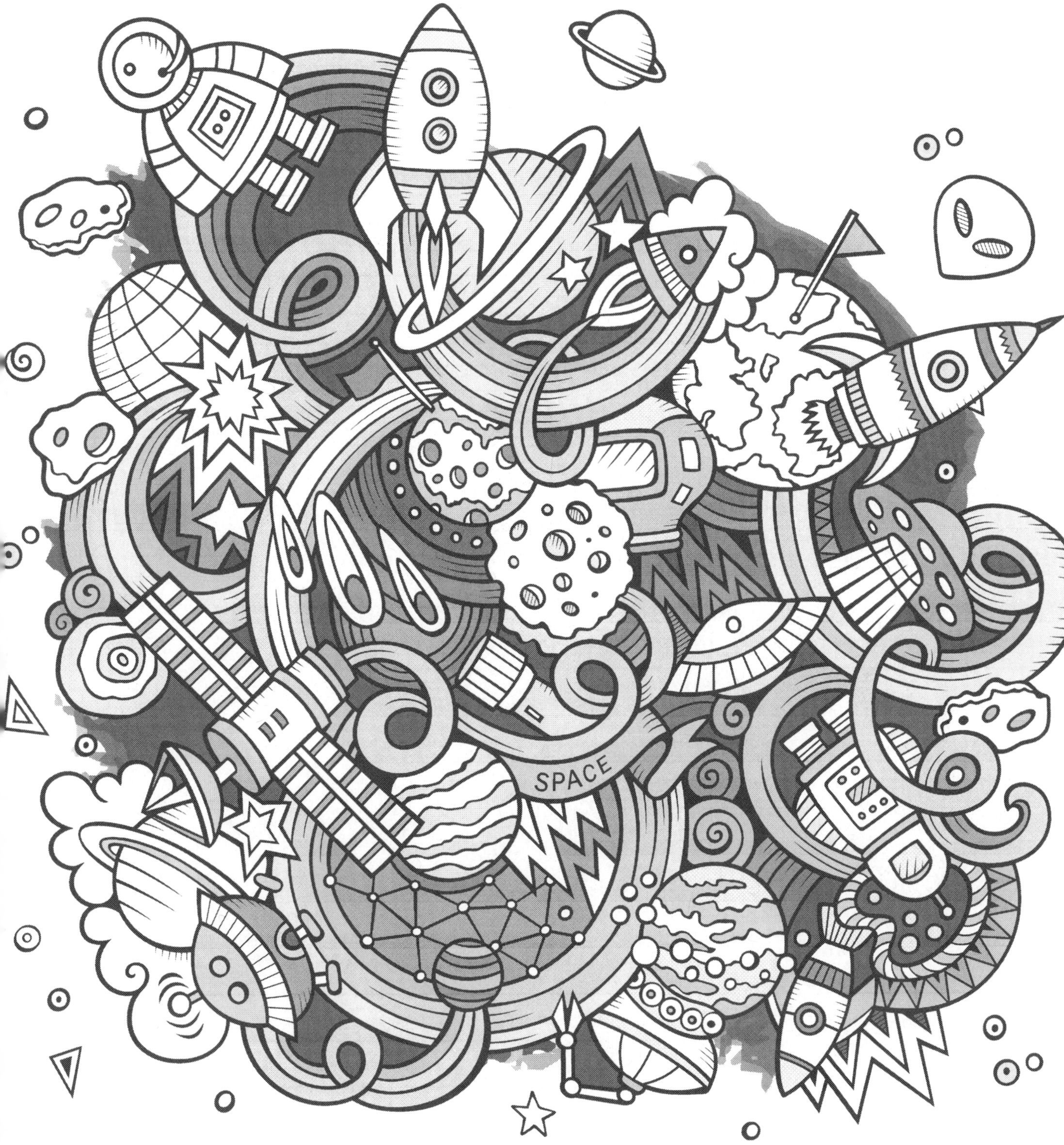
SPACE

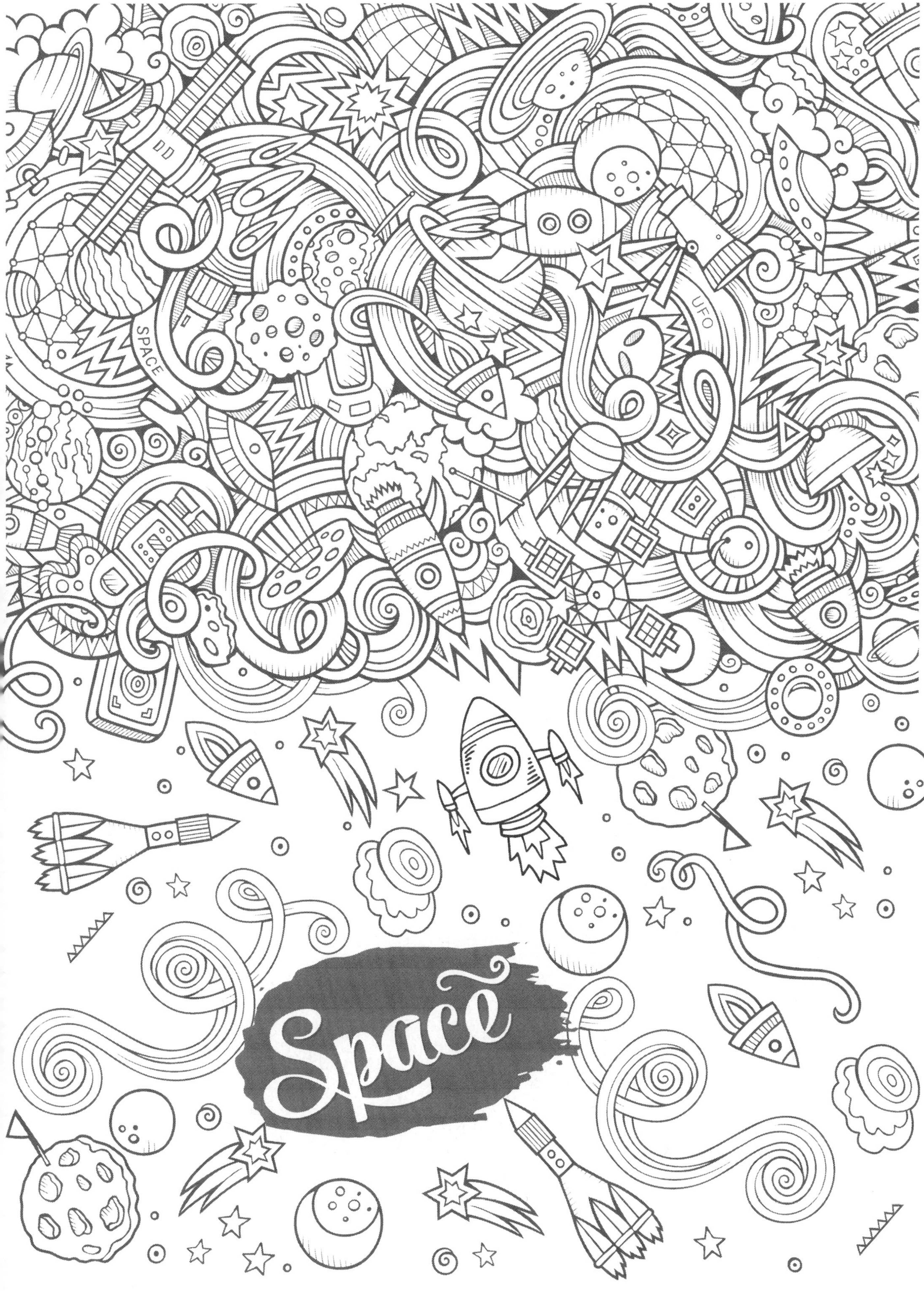
SPACE
UFO
Space

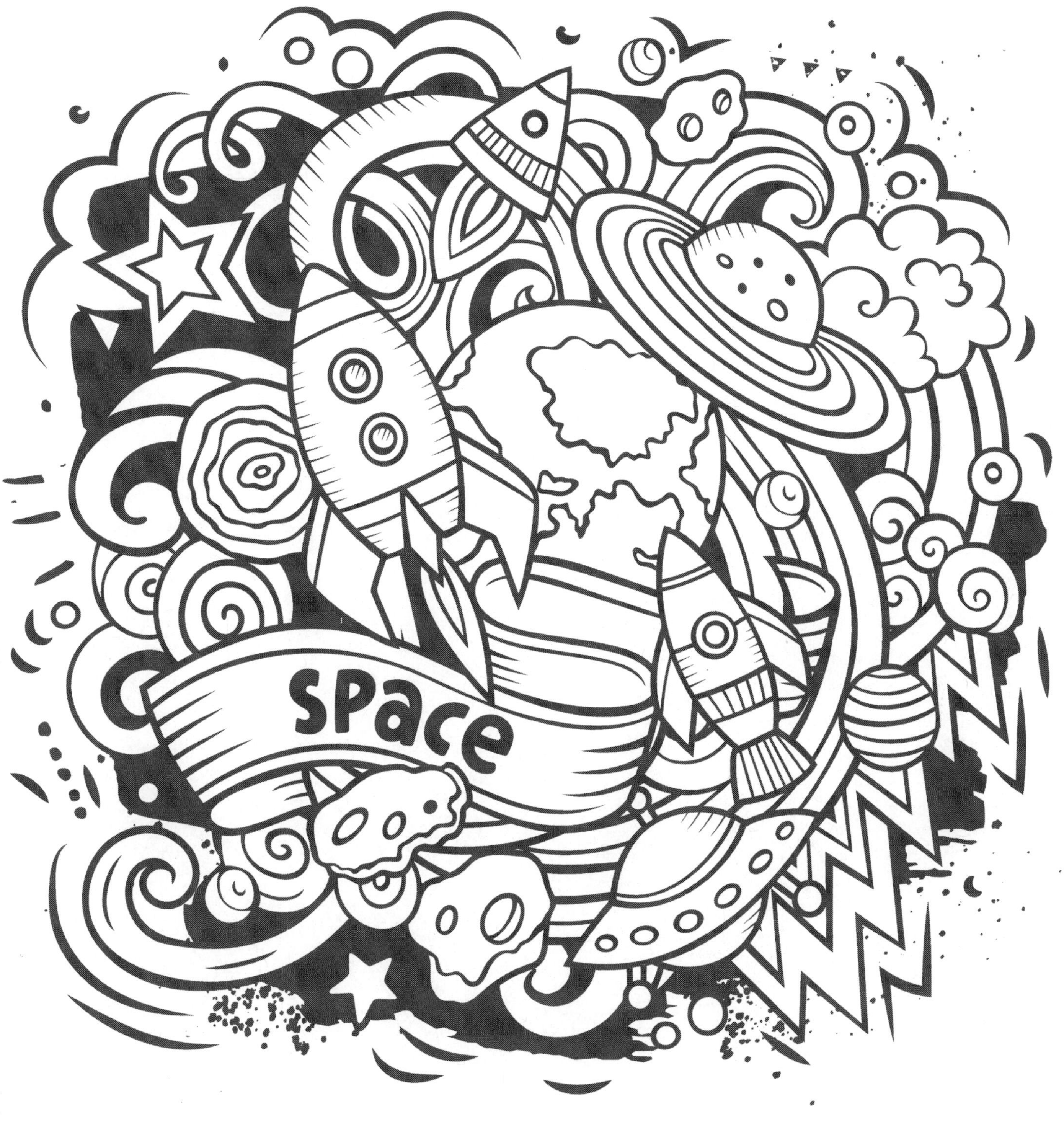
space

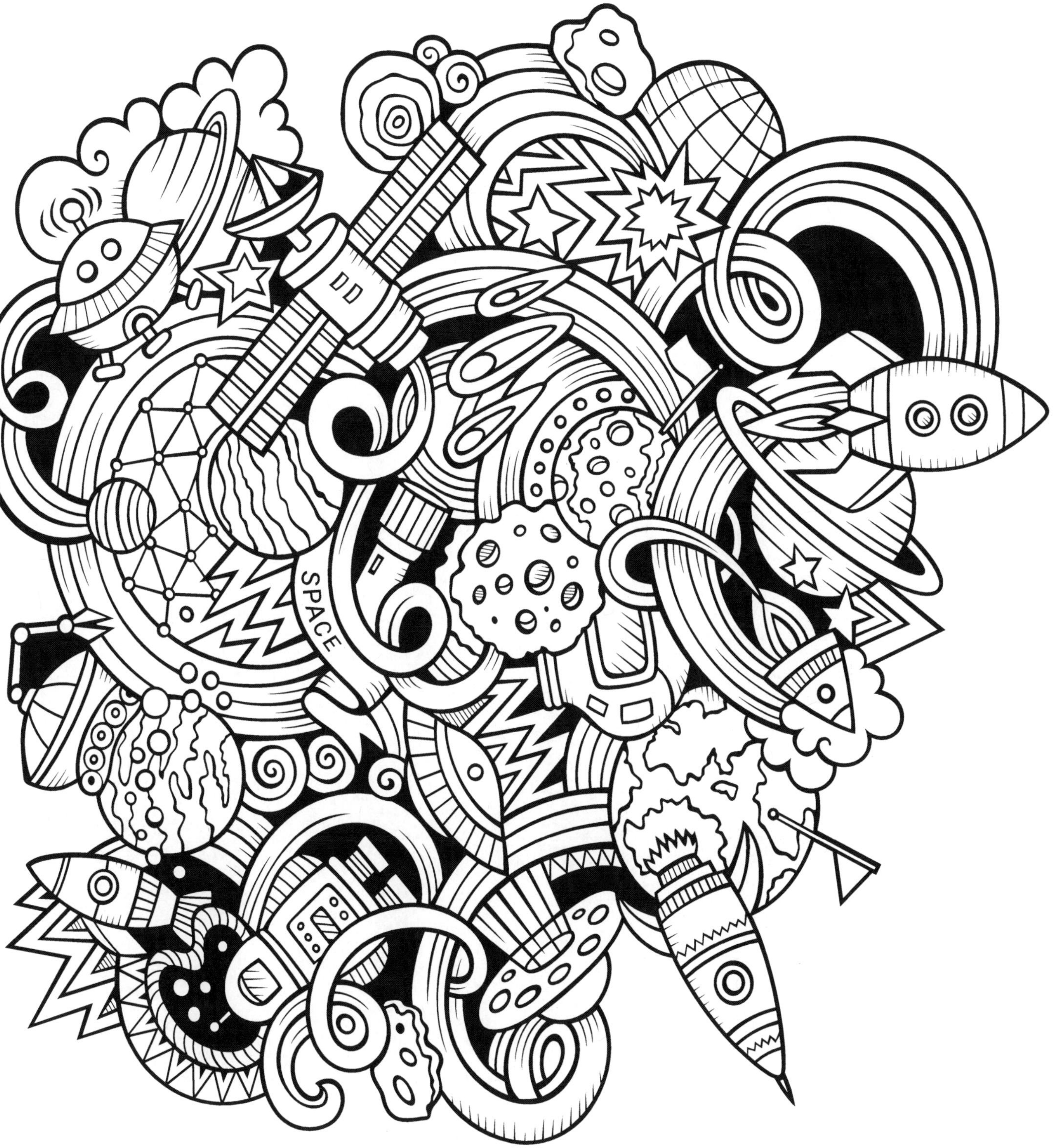
SPACE

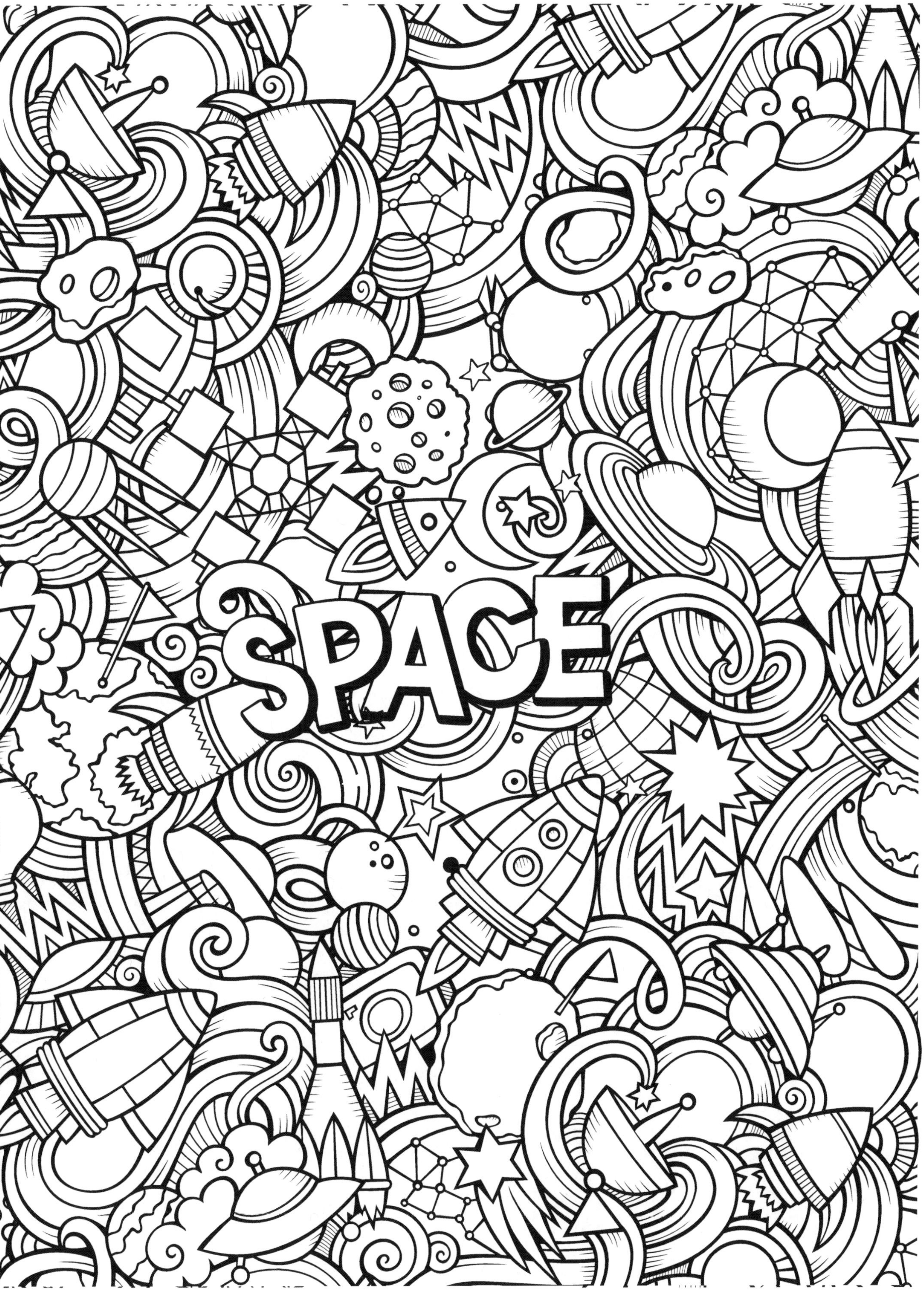
SPACE

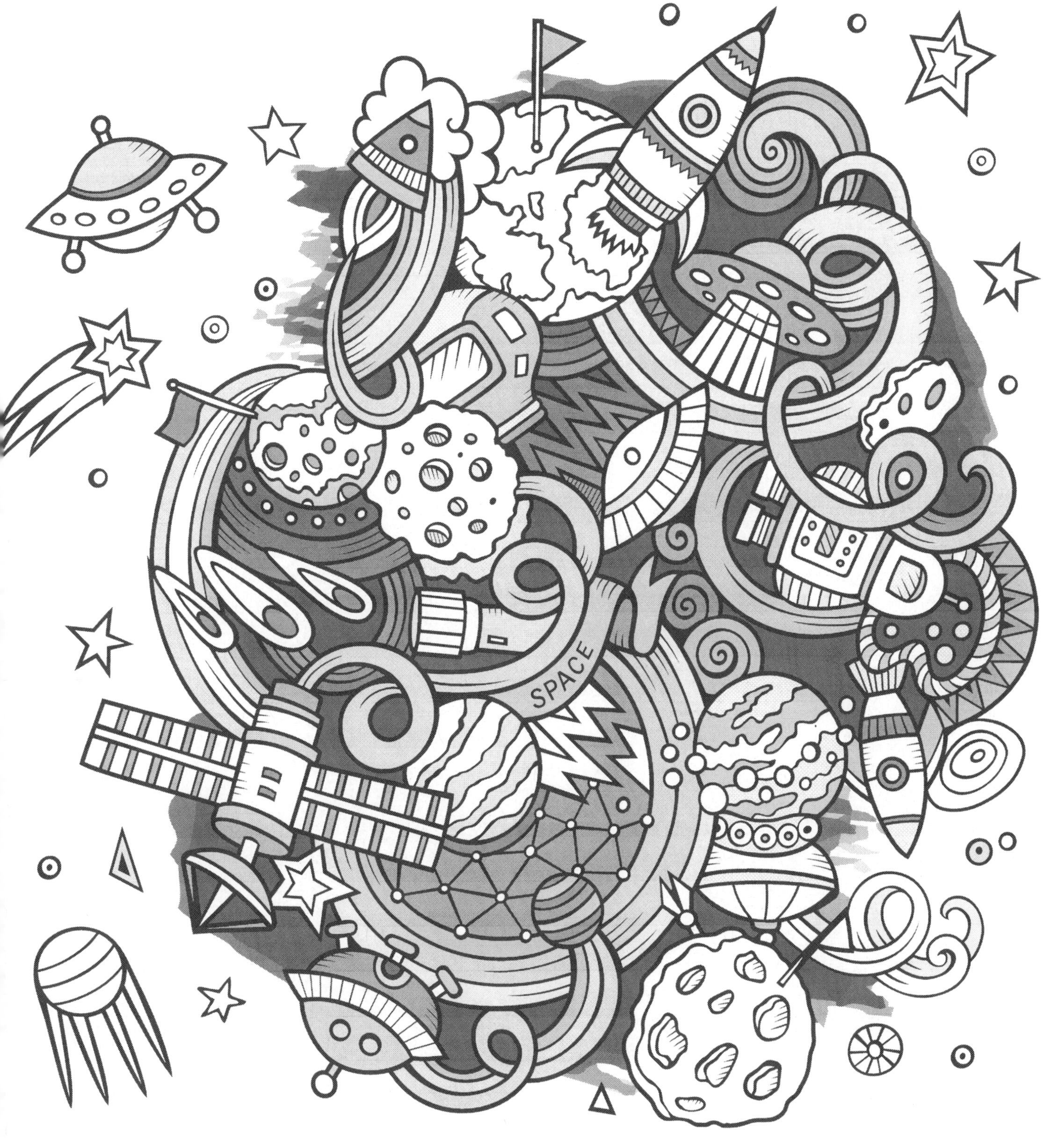
SPACE

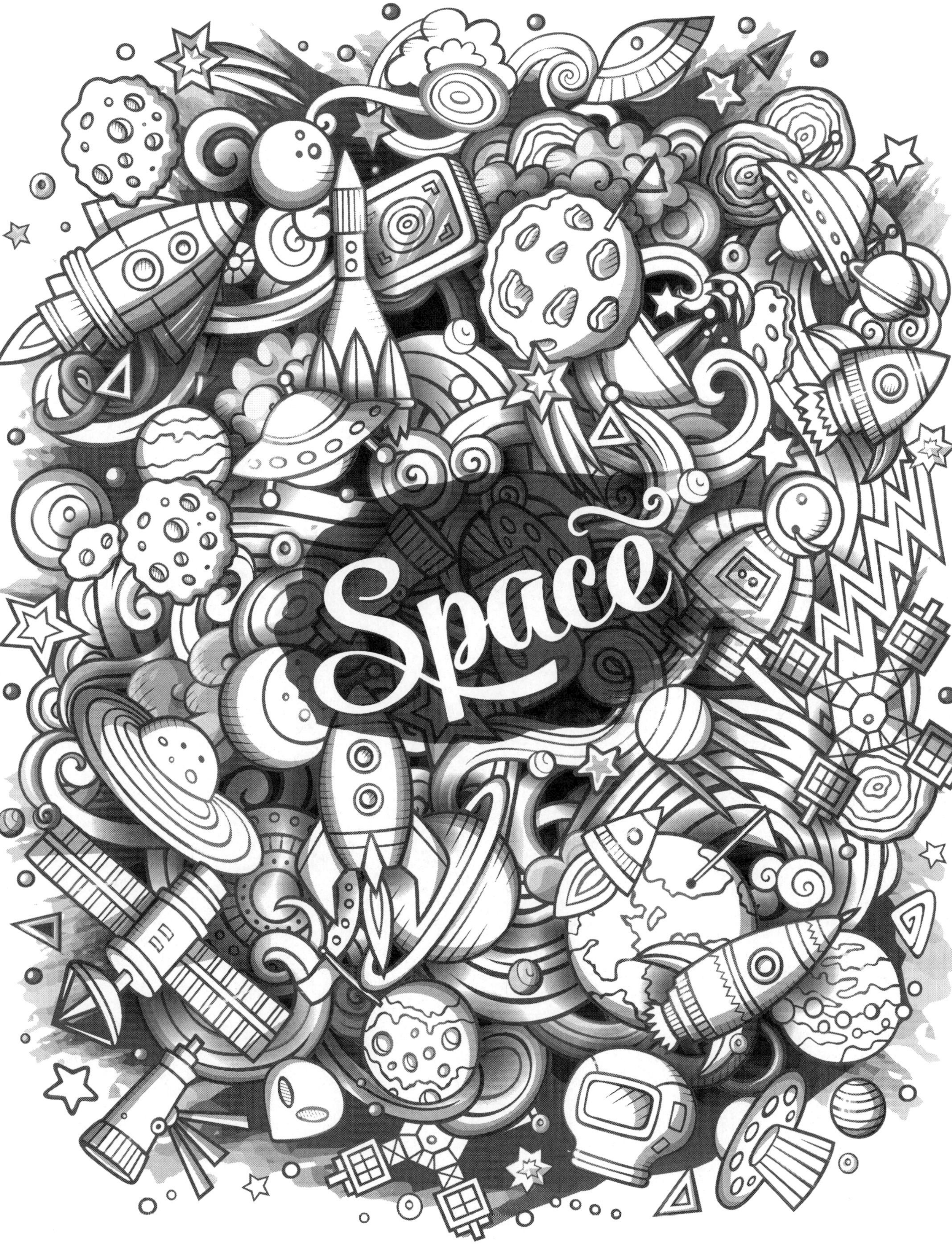
Space

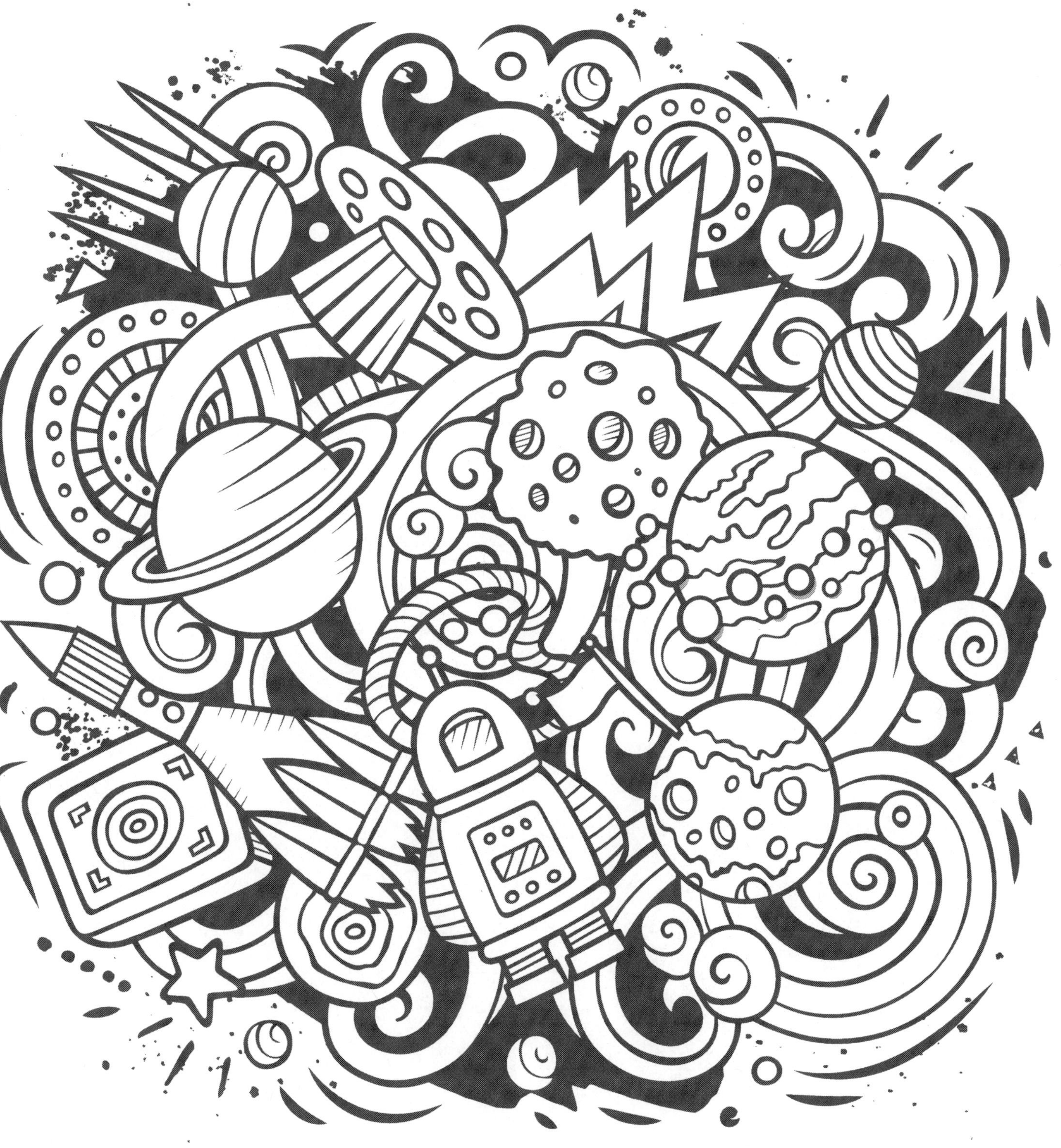

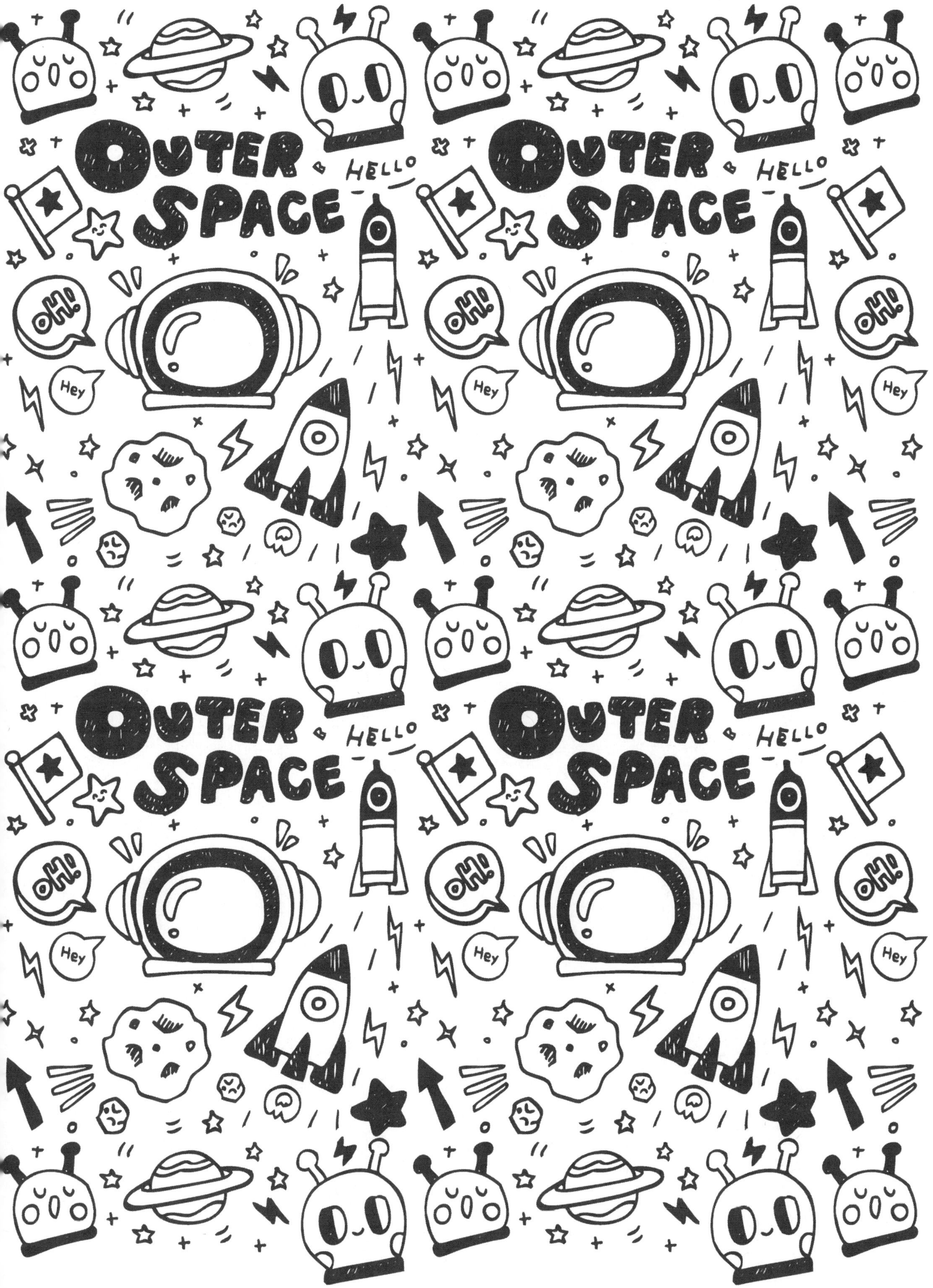
OUTER SPACE
HELLO
OH!
Hey
OUTER SPACE
HELLO
OH!
Hey
OUTER SPACE
HELLO
OH!
Hey
OUTER SPACE
HELLO
OH!
Hey

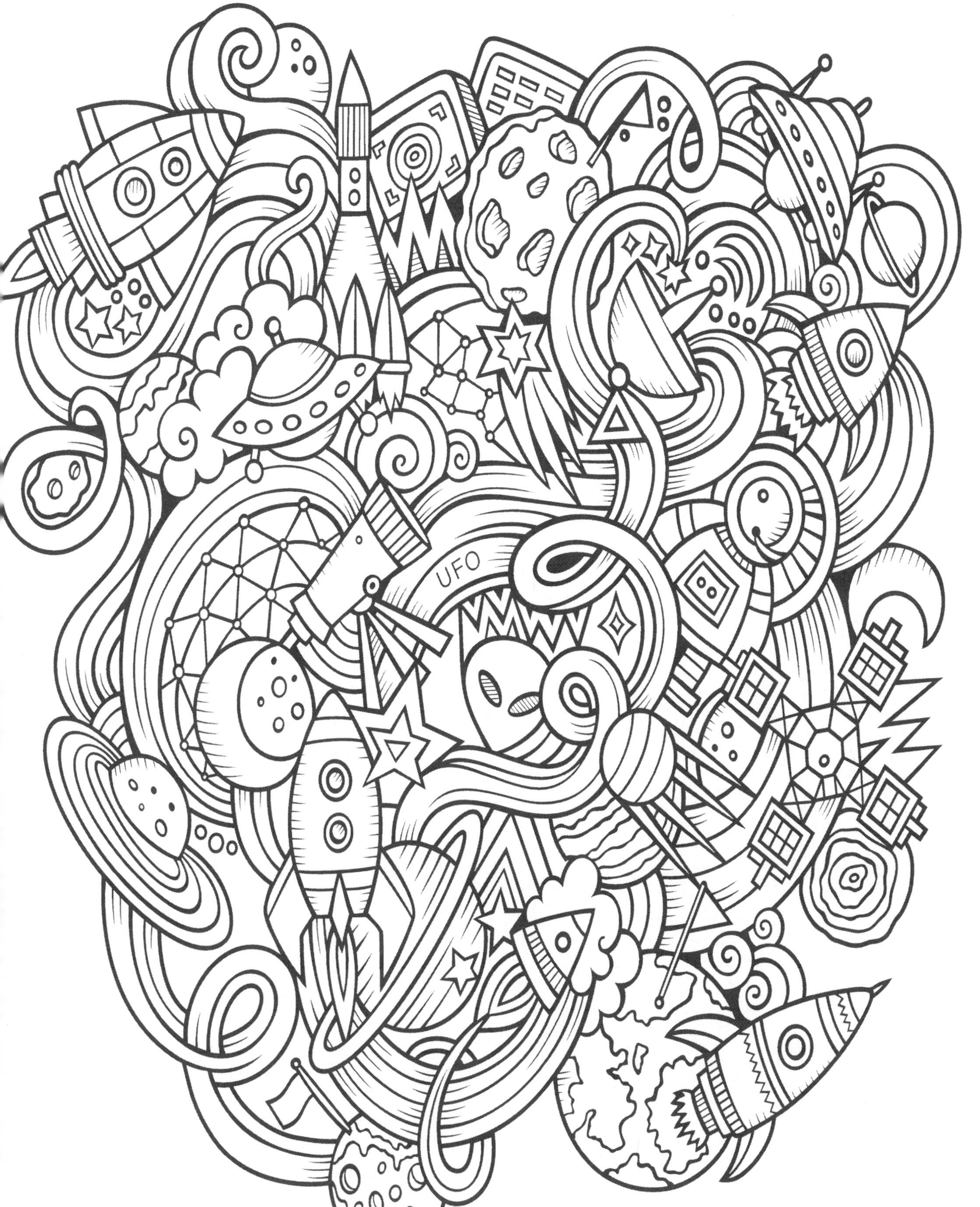
UFO

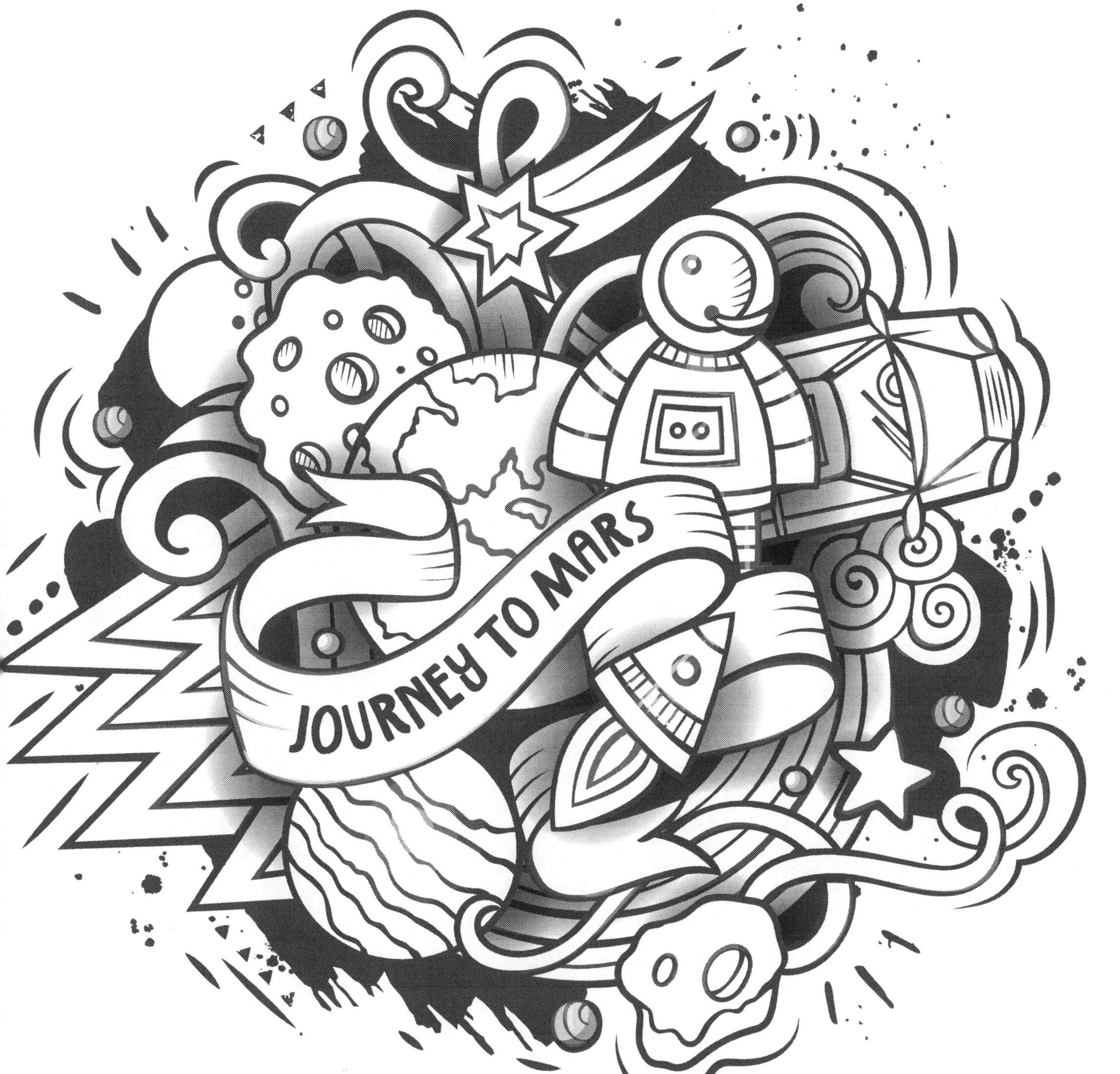
JOURNEY TO MARS

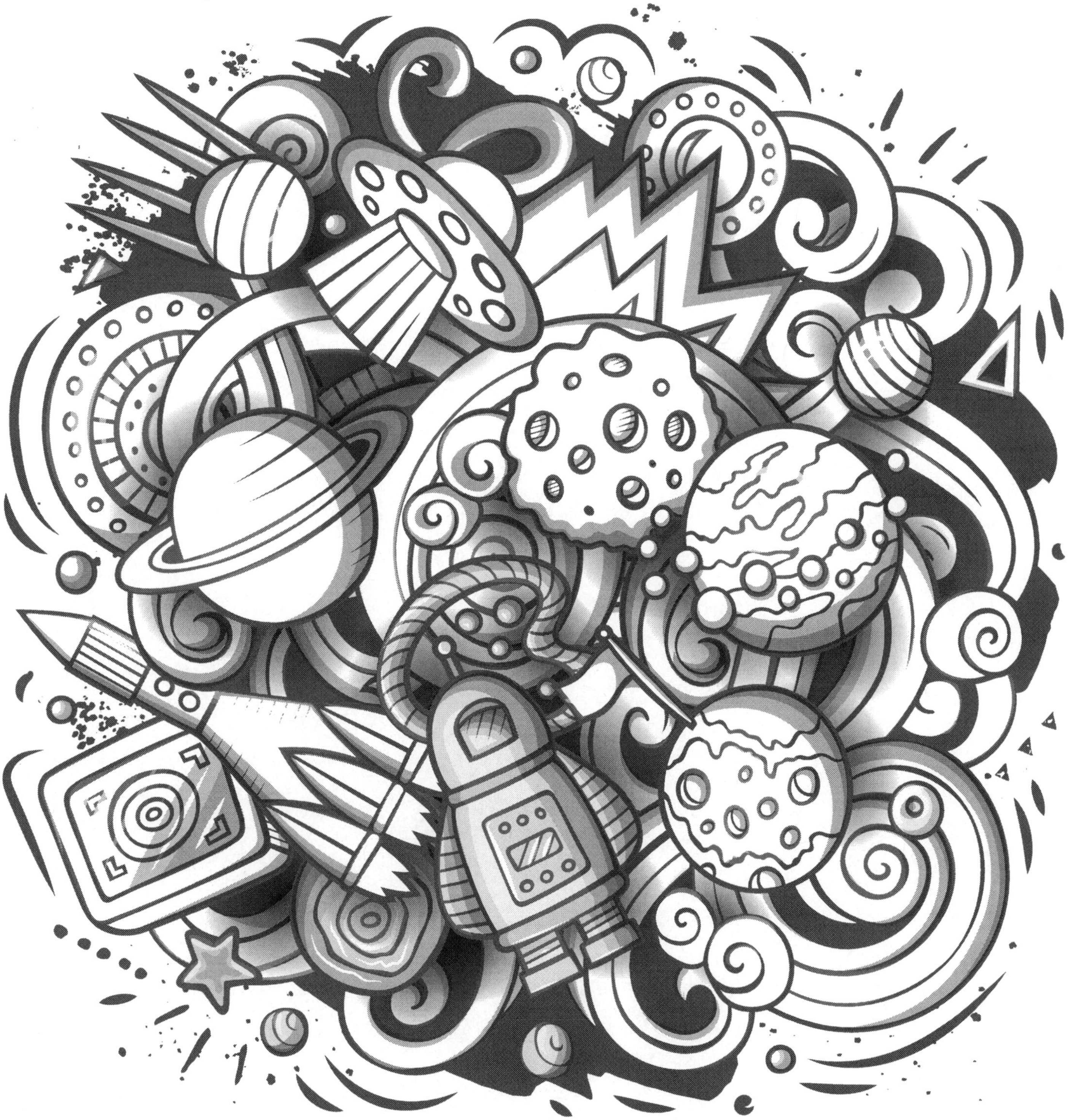

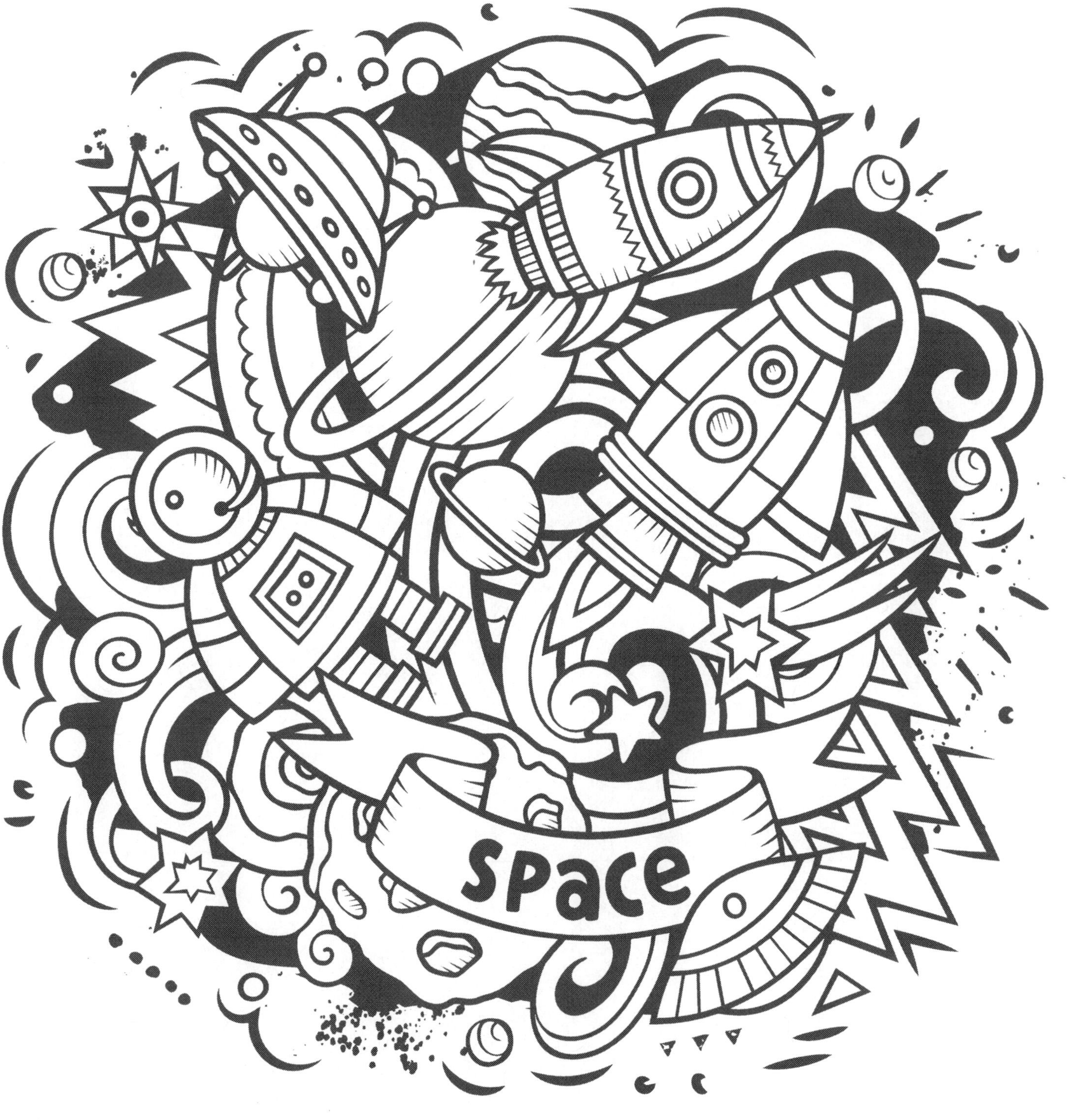
SPACE

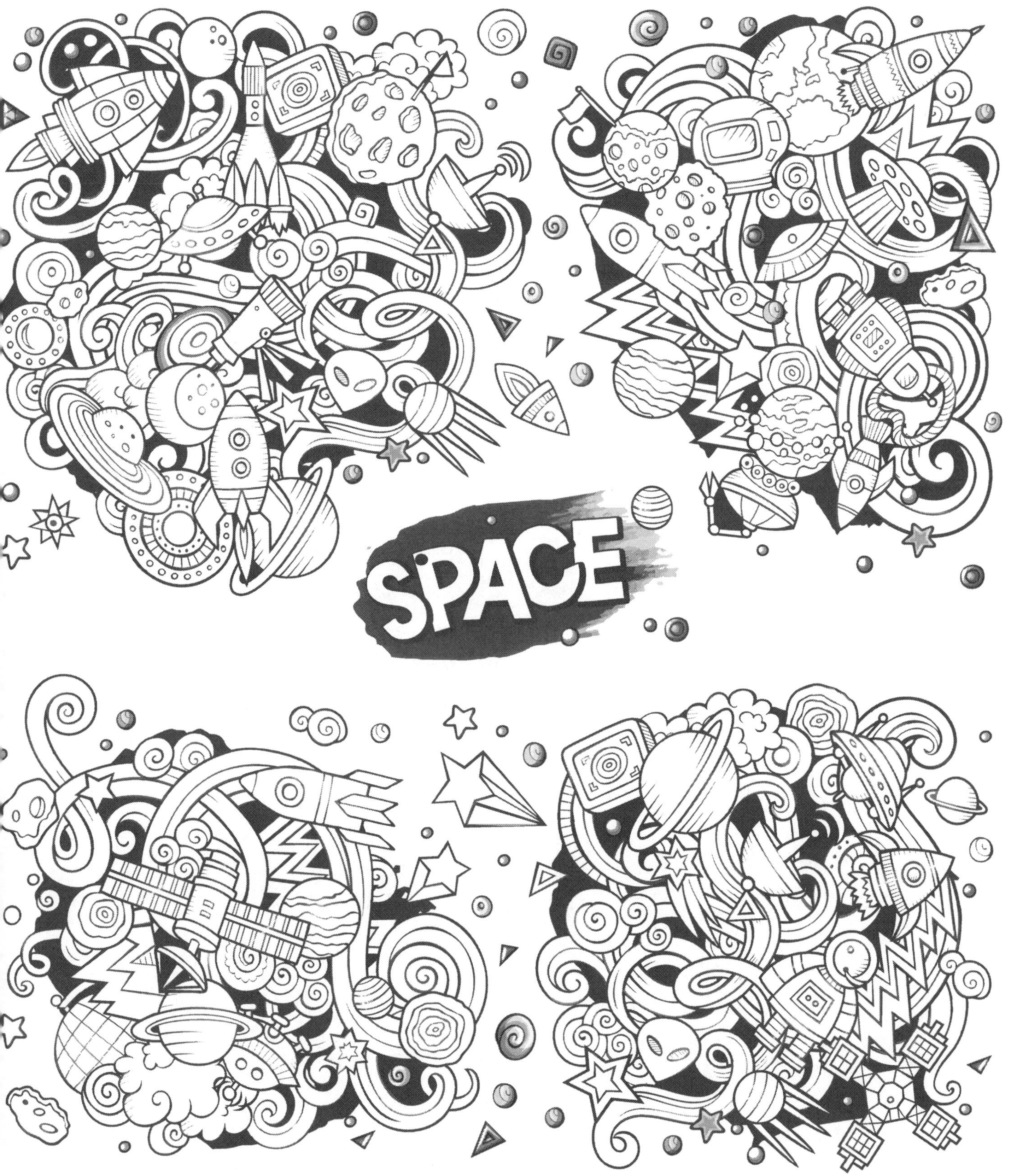
SPACE

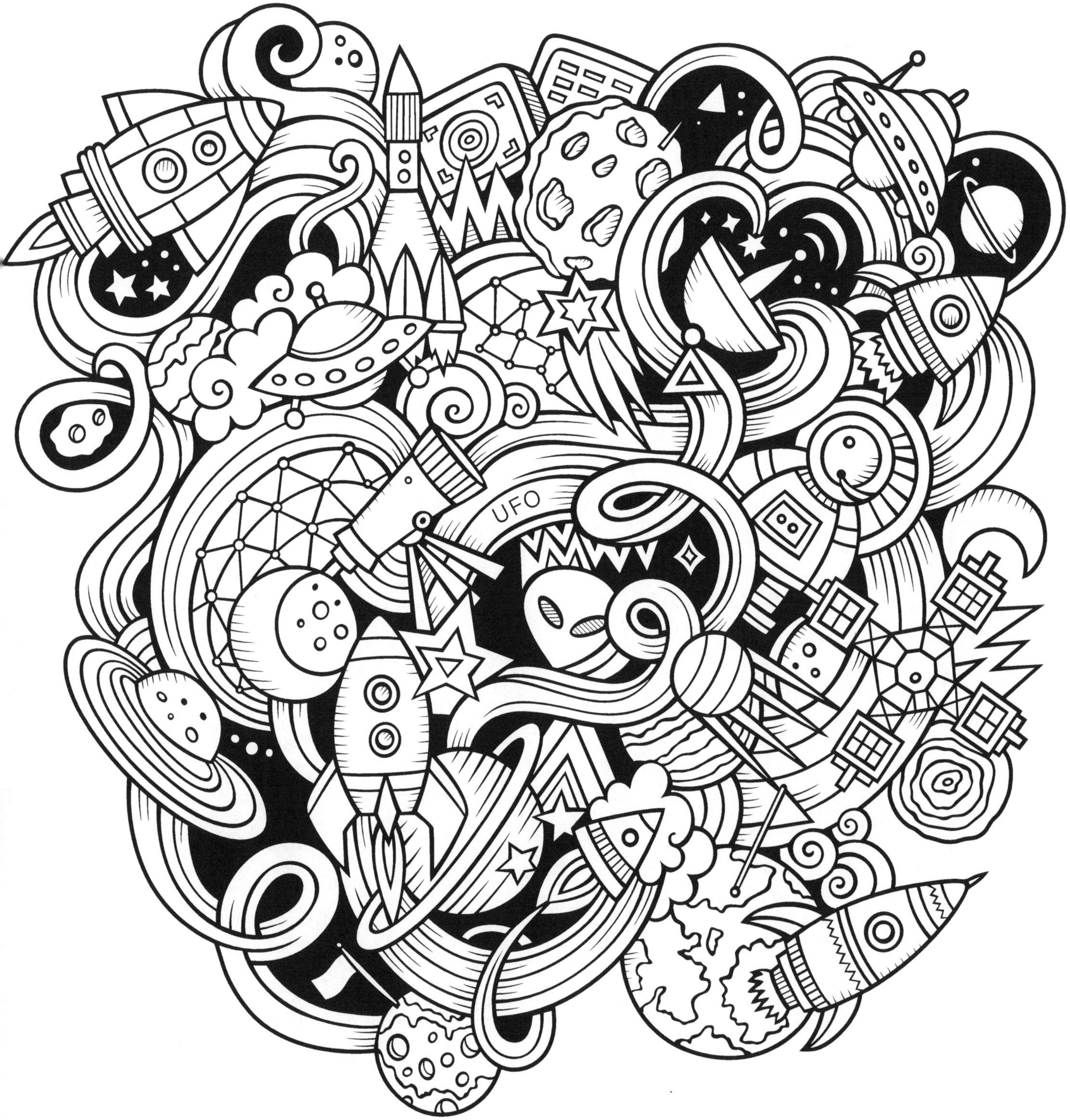
UFO

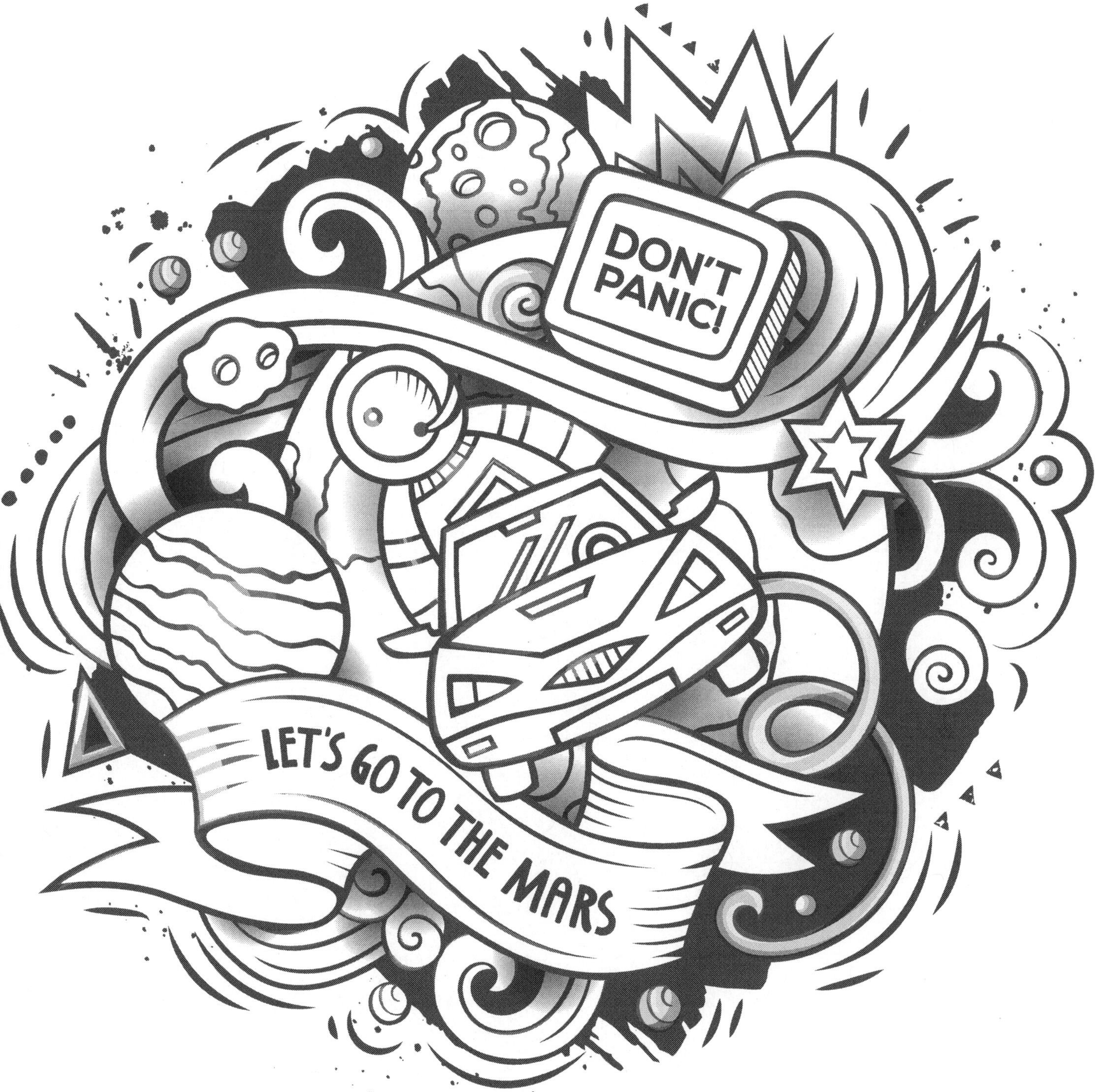
DON'T PANIC!
LET'S GO TO THE MARS

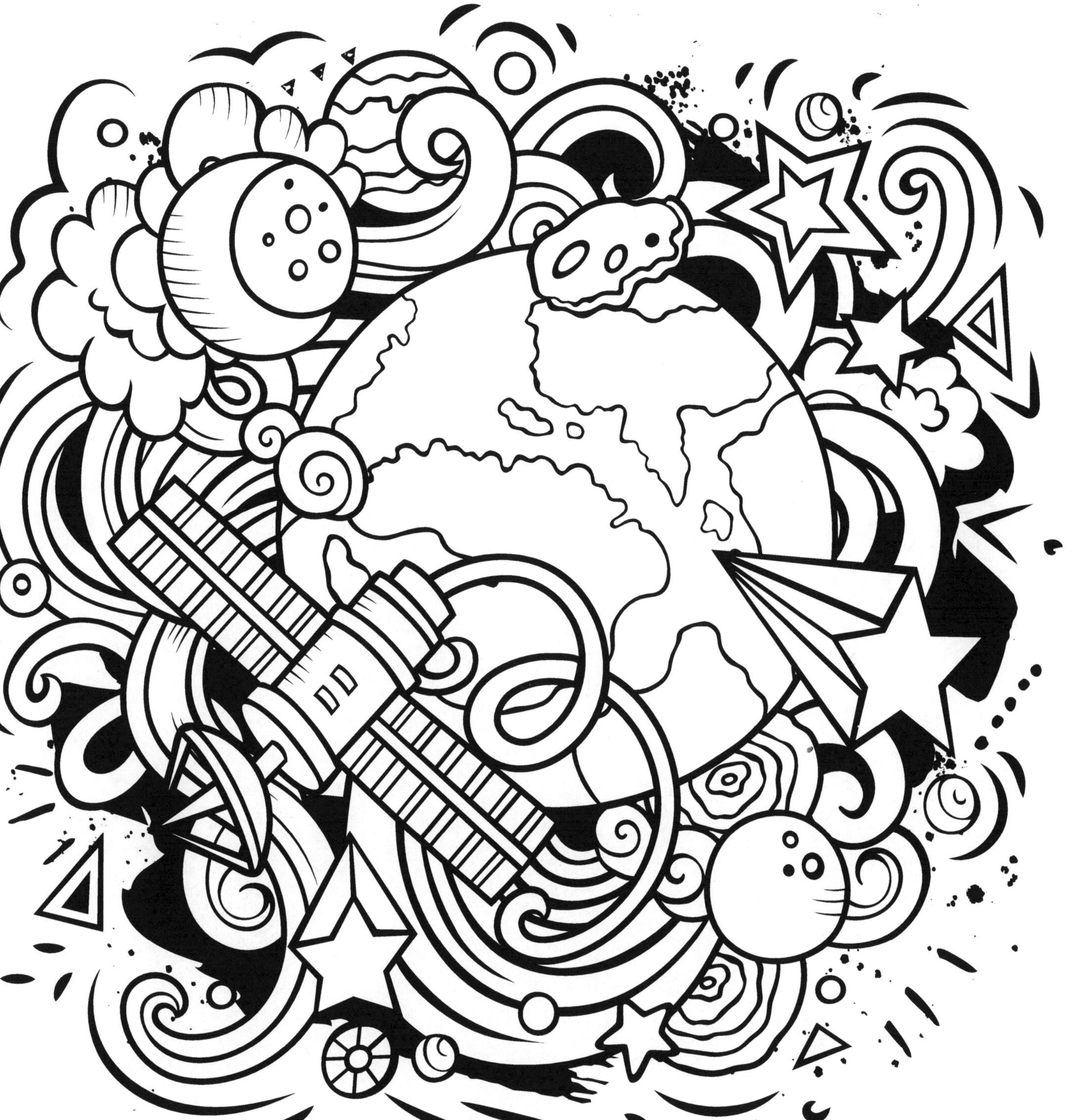

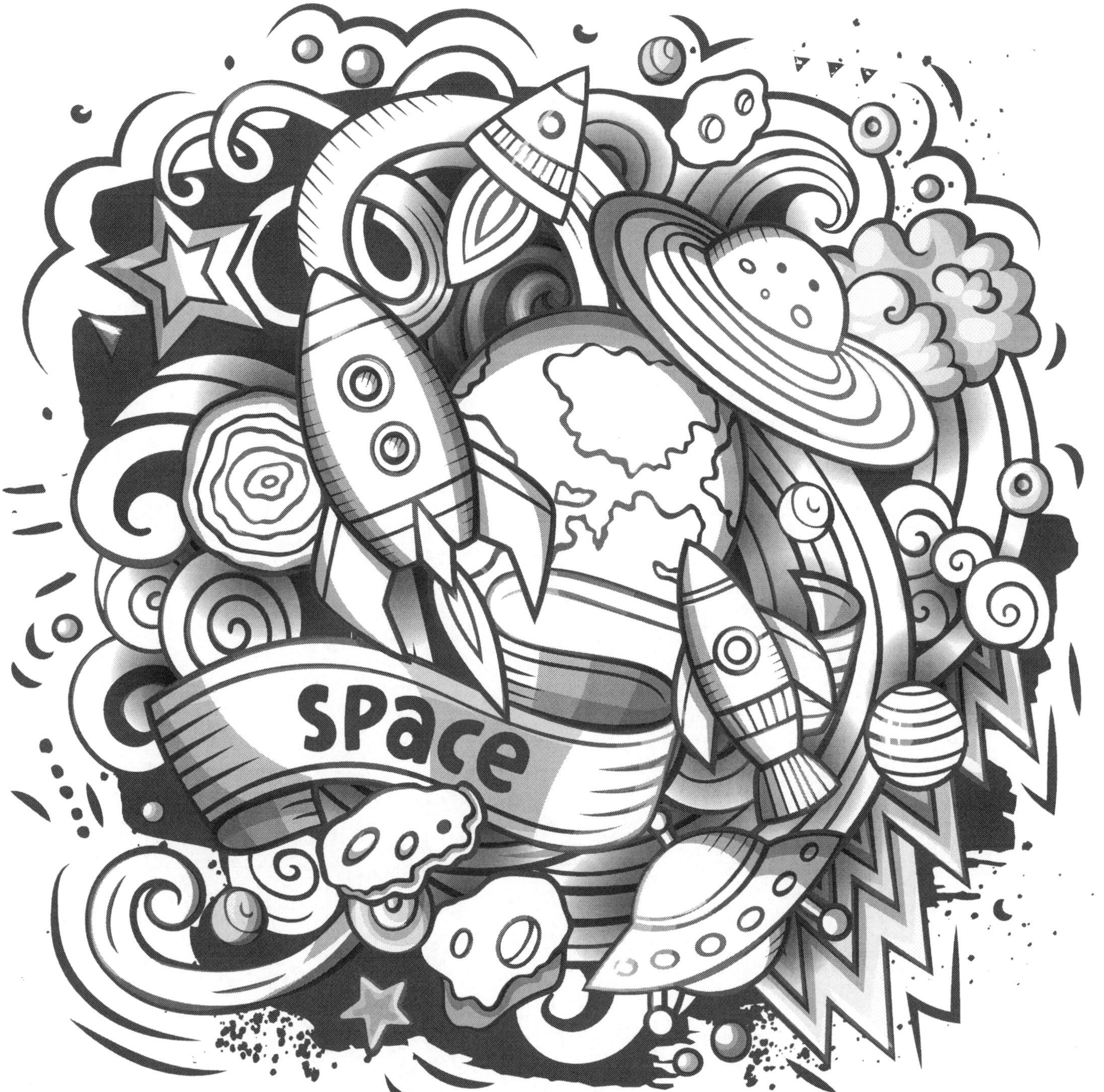
SPace

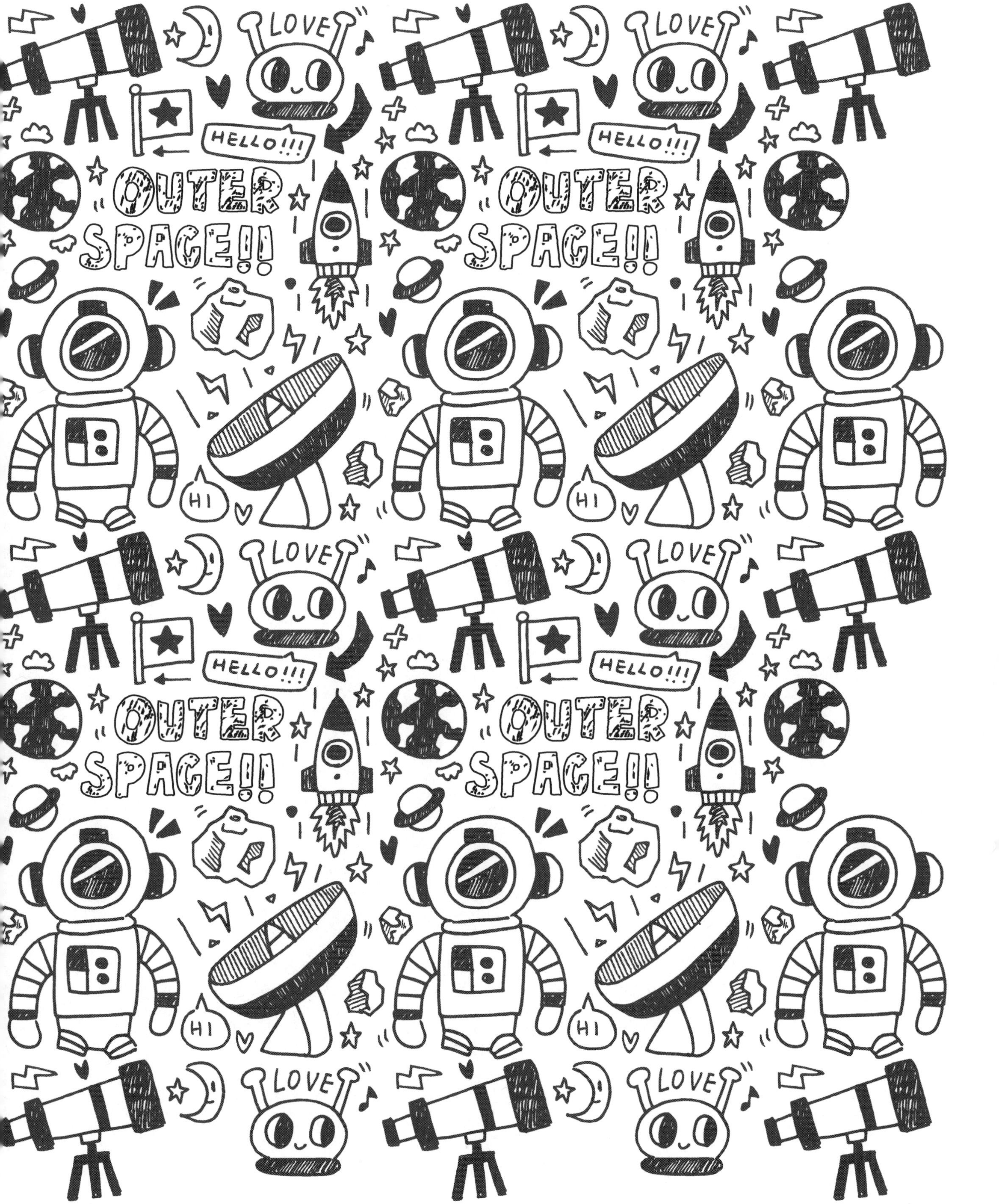
LOVE
HELLO!!!
OUTER SPACE!!
HI

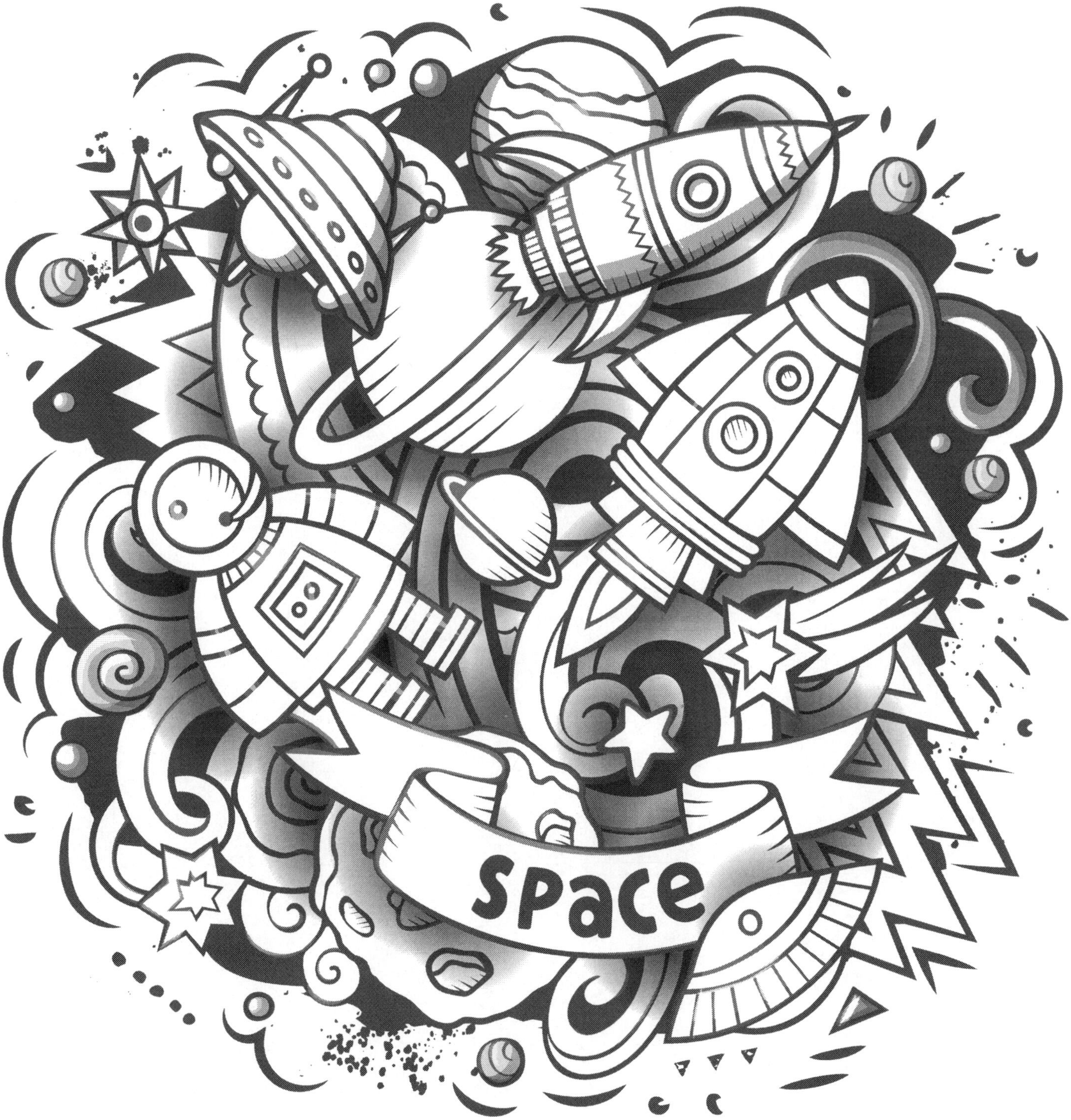
SPACE

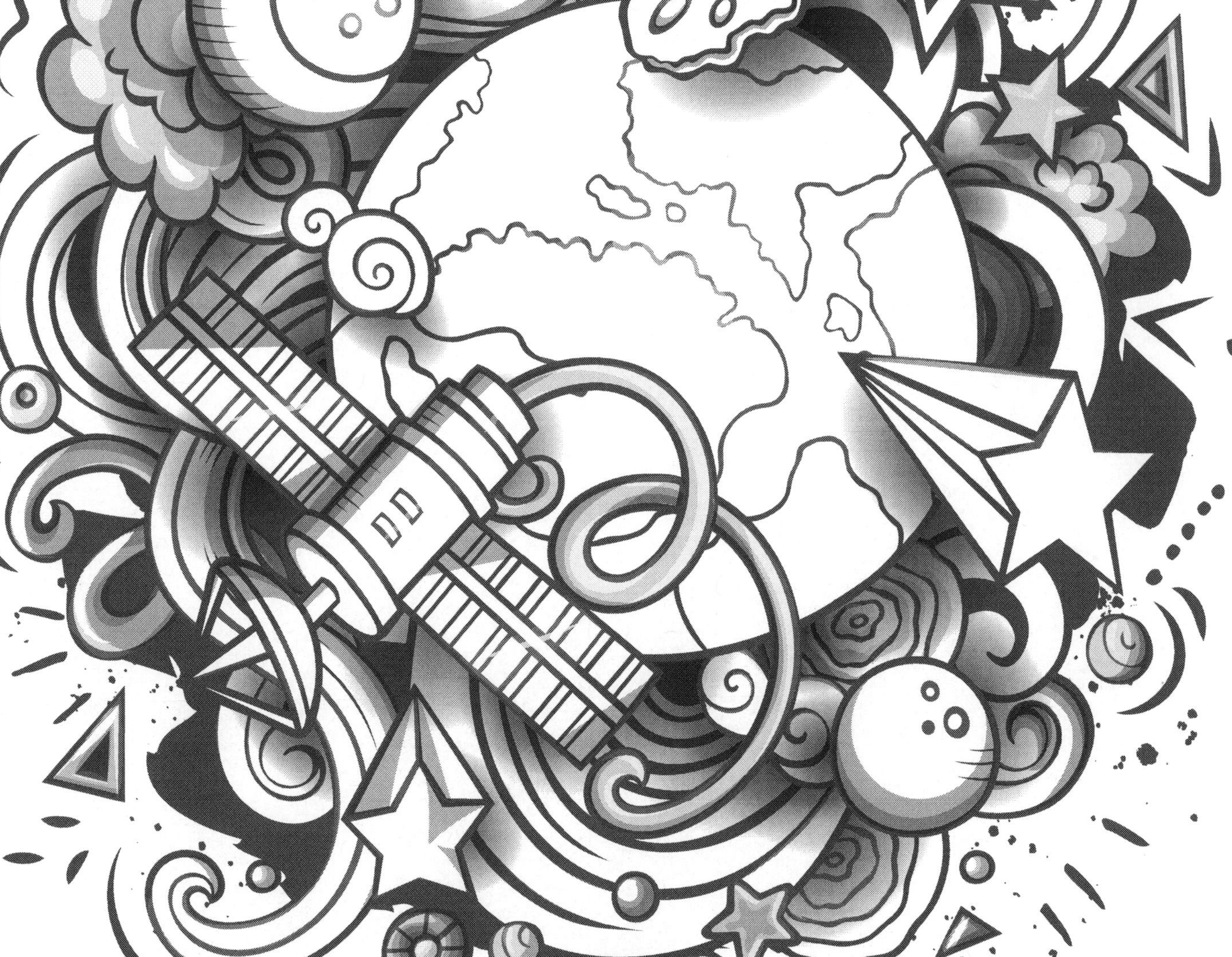

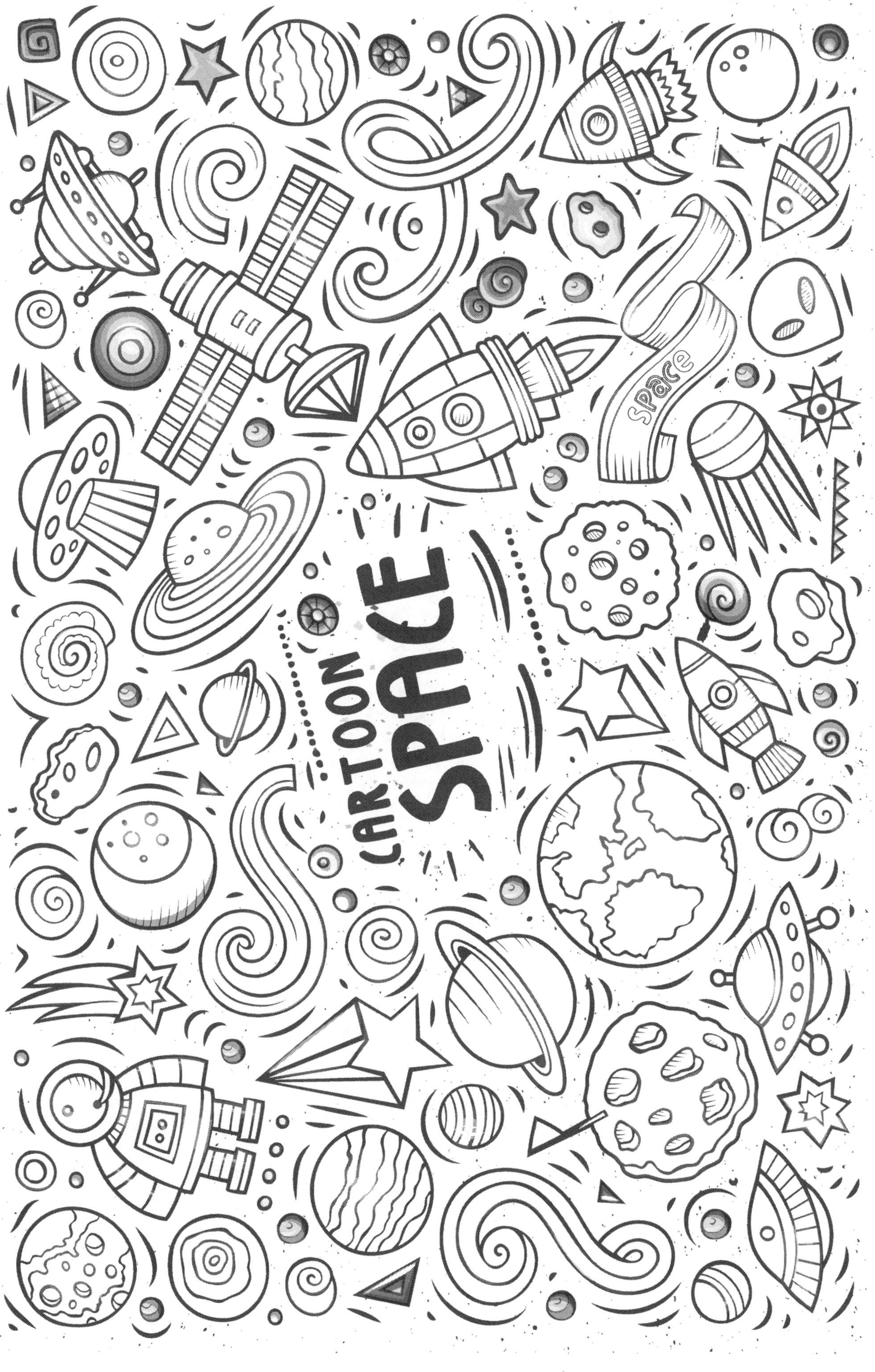
SPACE
CARTOON
SPACE

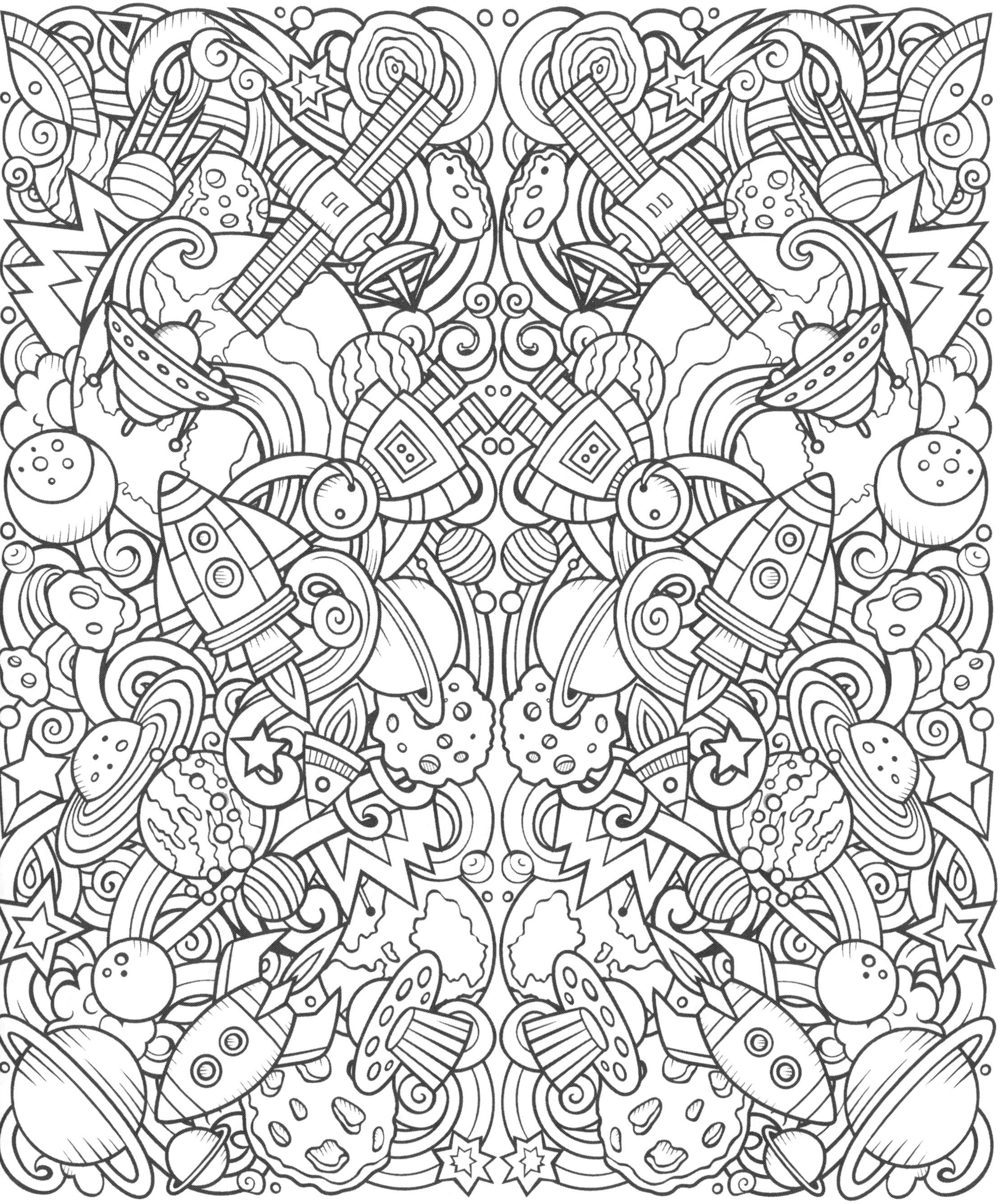

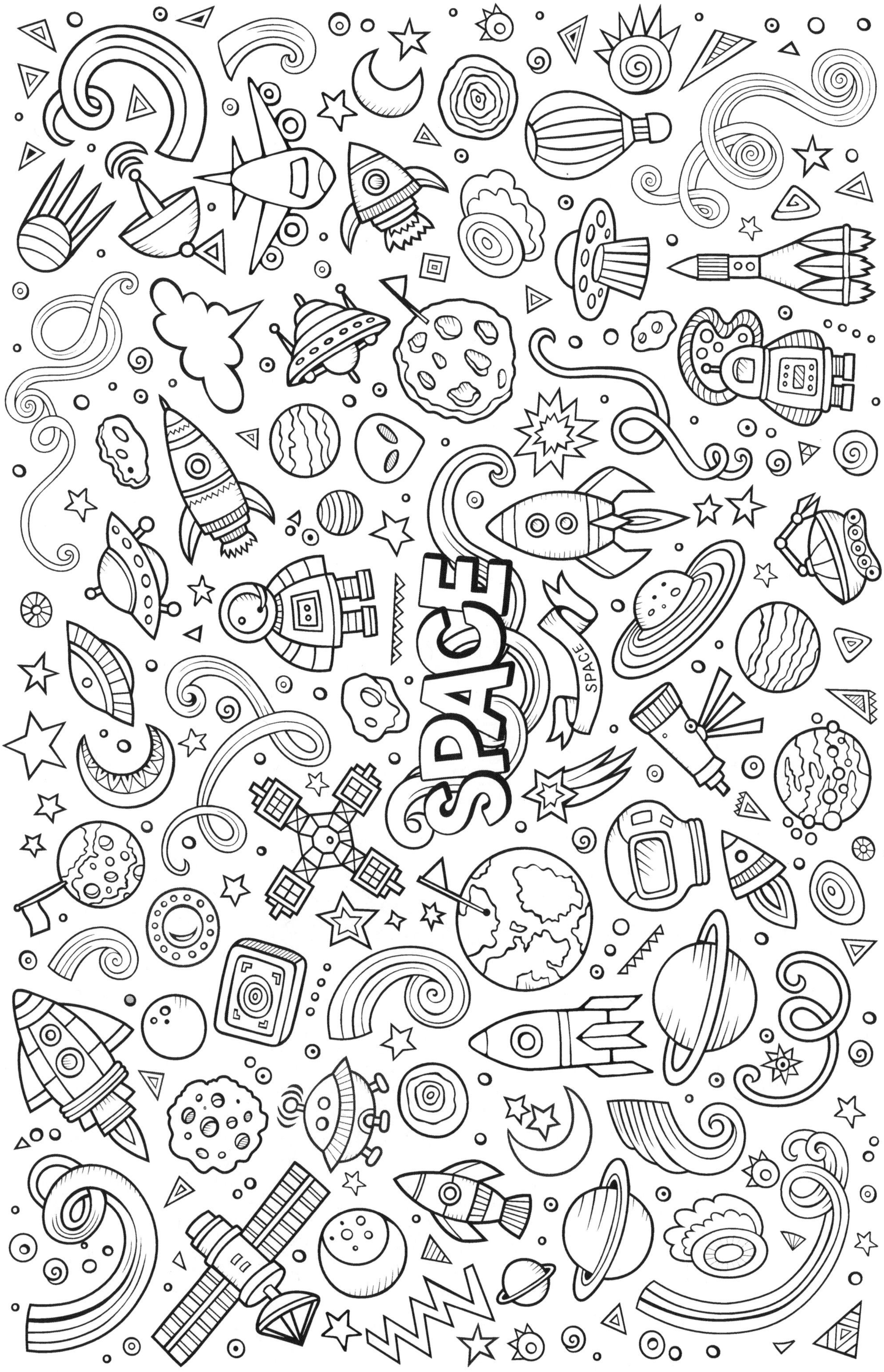
SPACE
SPACE

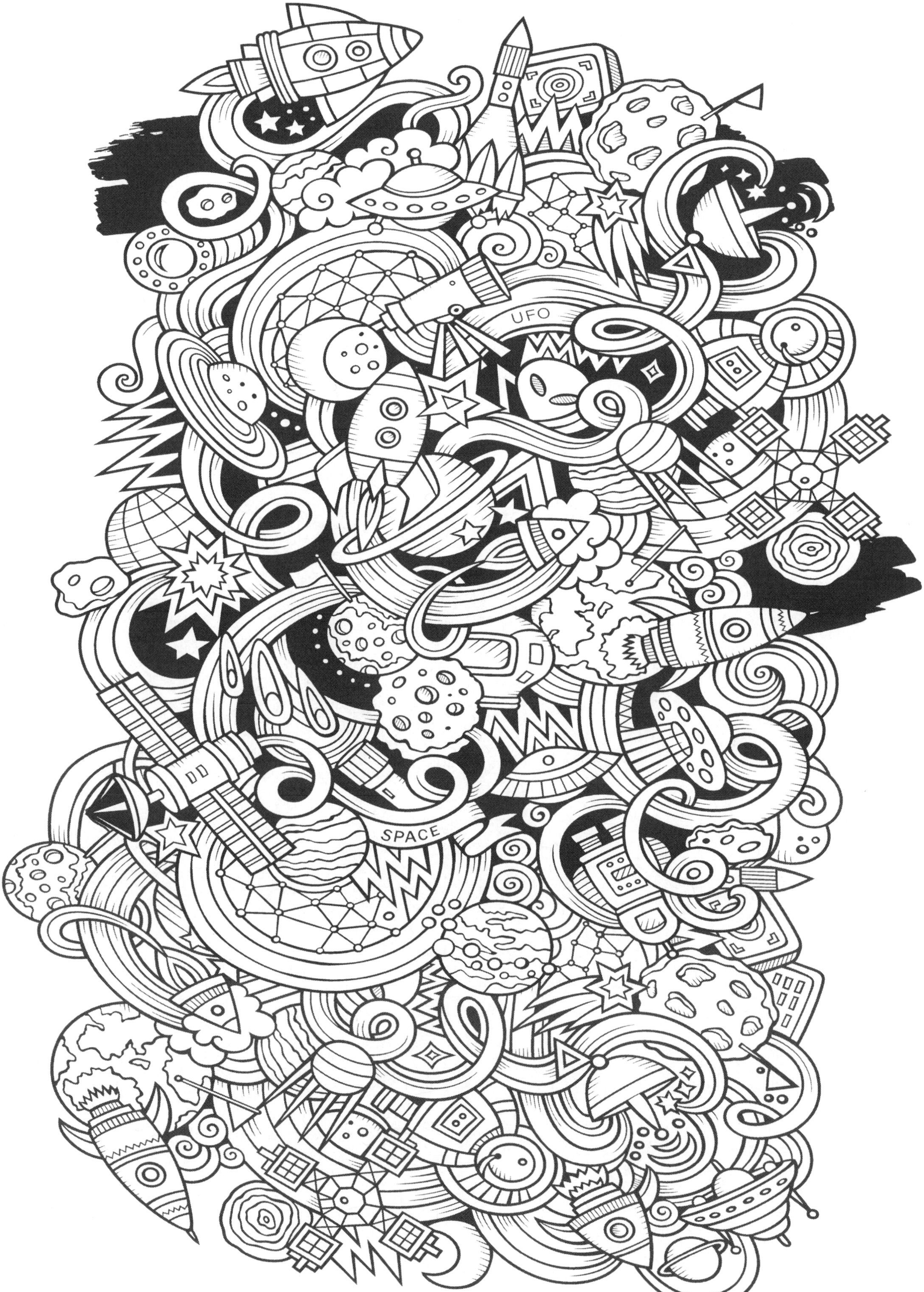
UFO
SPACE

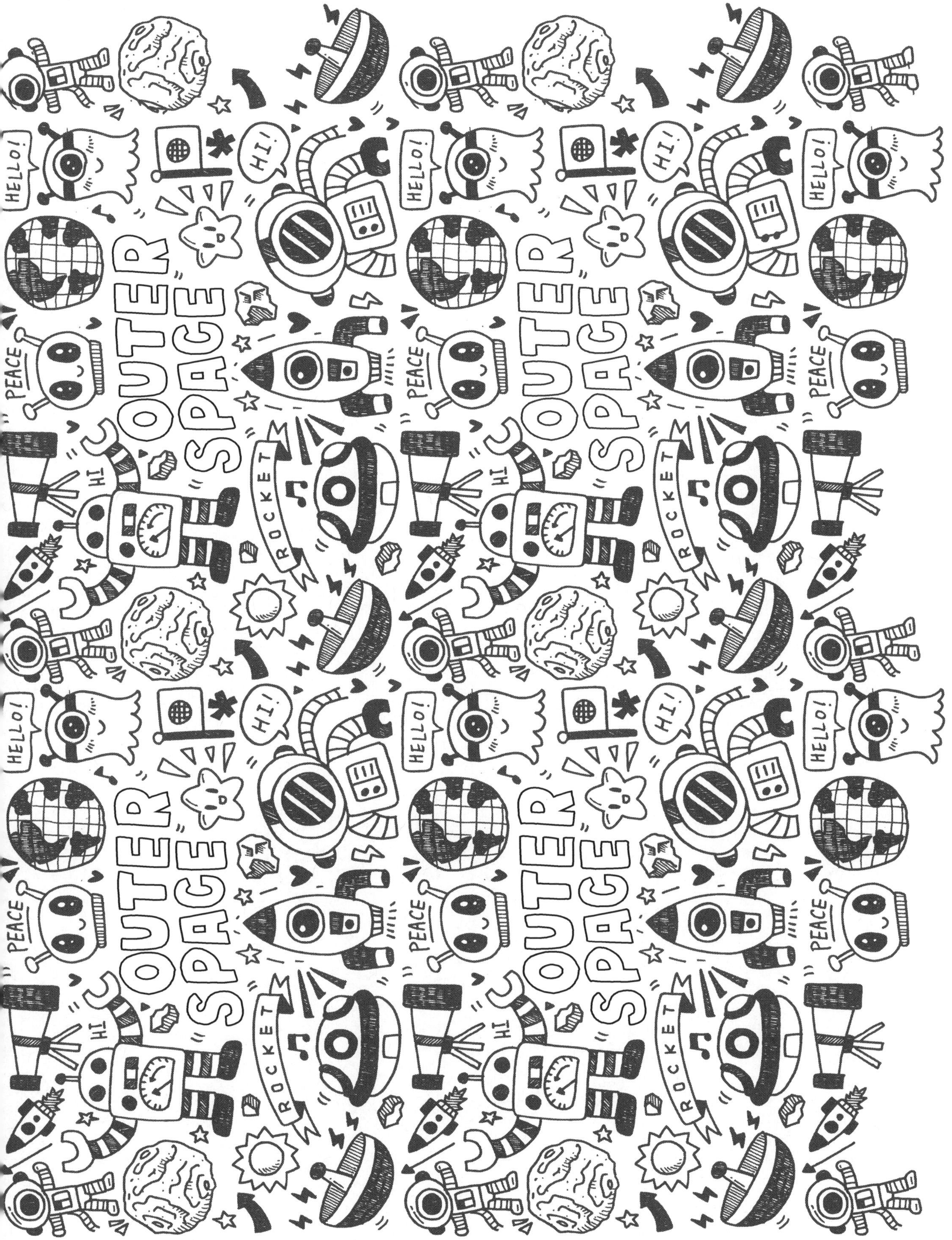
HELLO!
HI!
OUTER SPACE
PEACE
HI
ROCKET

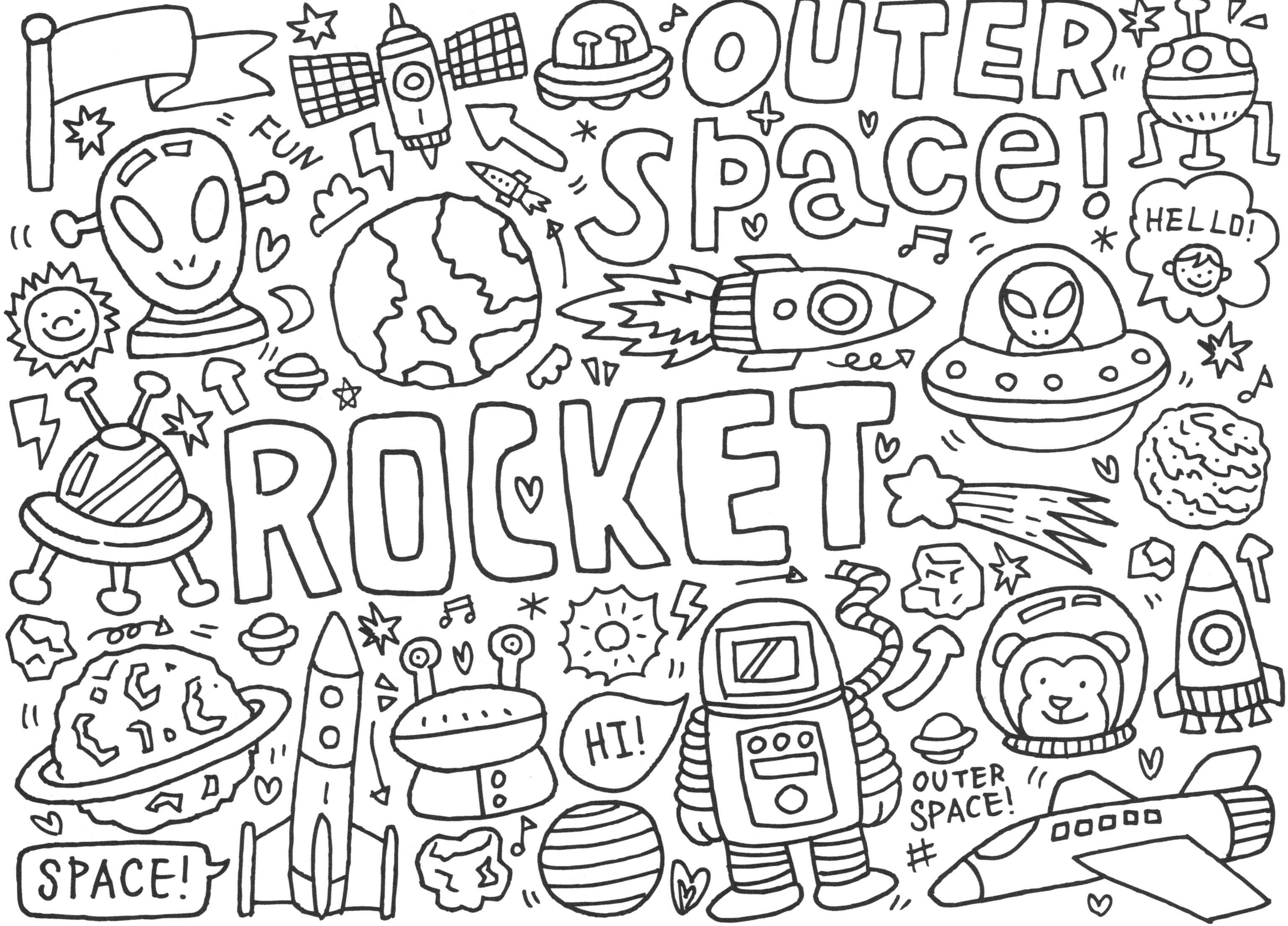
OUTER Space!
ROCKET
FUN
HELLO!
HI!
OUTER SPACE!
SPACE!

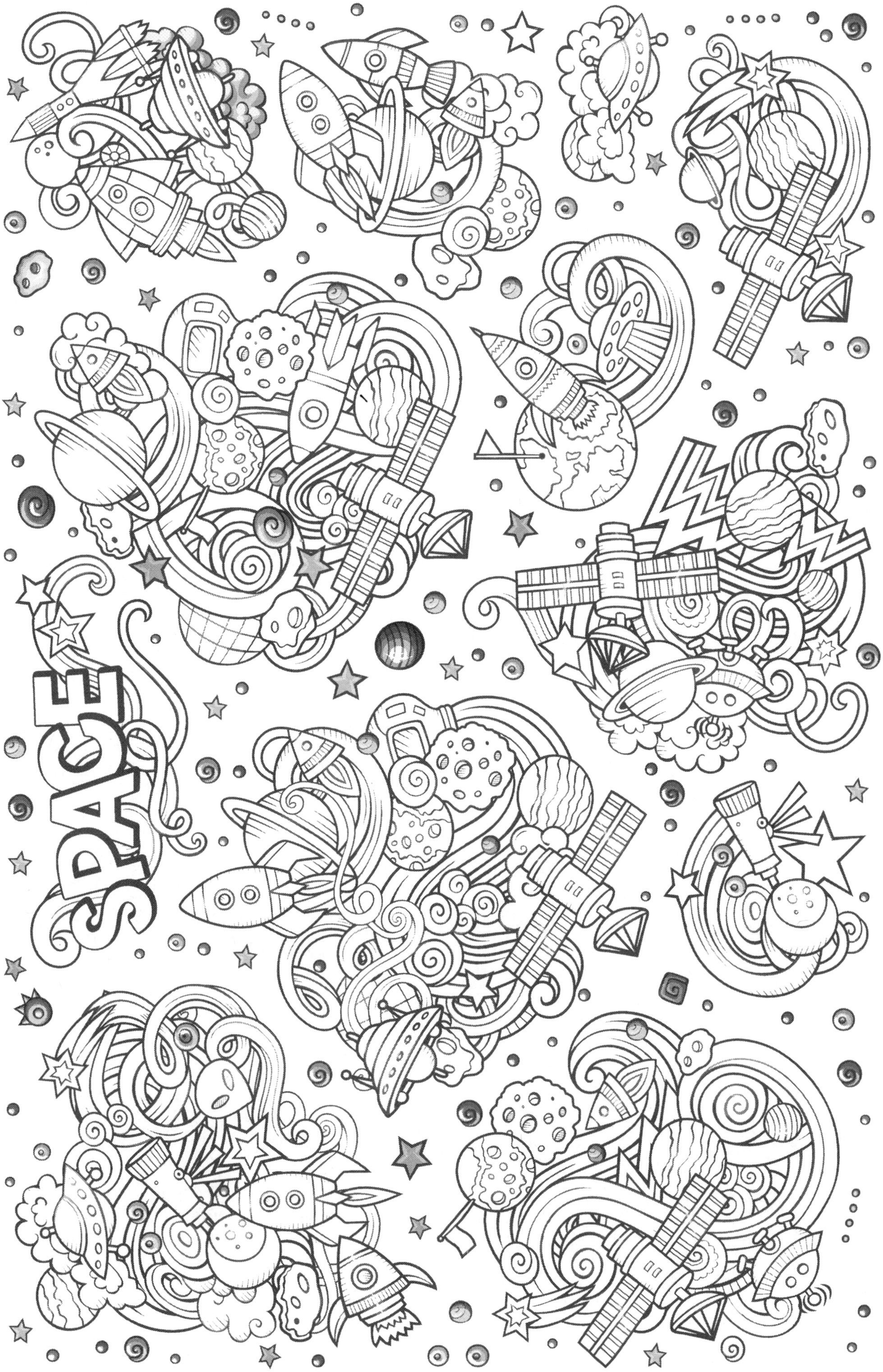
SPACE

OUTER
space!
ROCKET
SPACE!
HELLO!
HI!
FUN
OUTER SPACE!

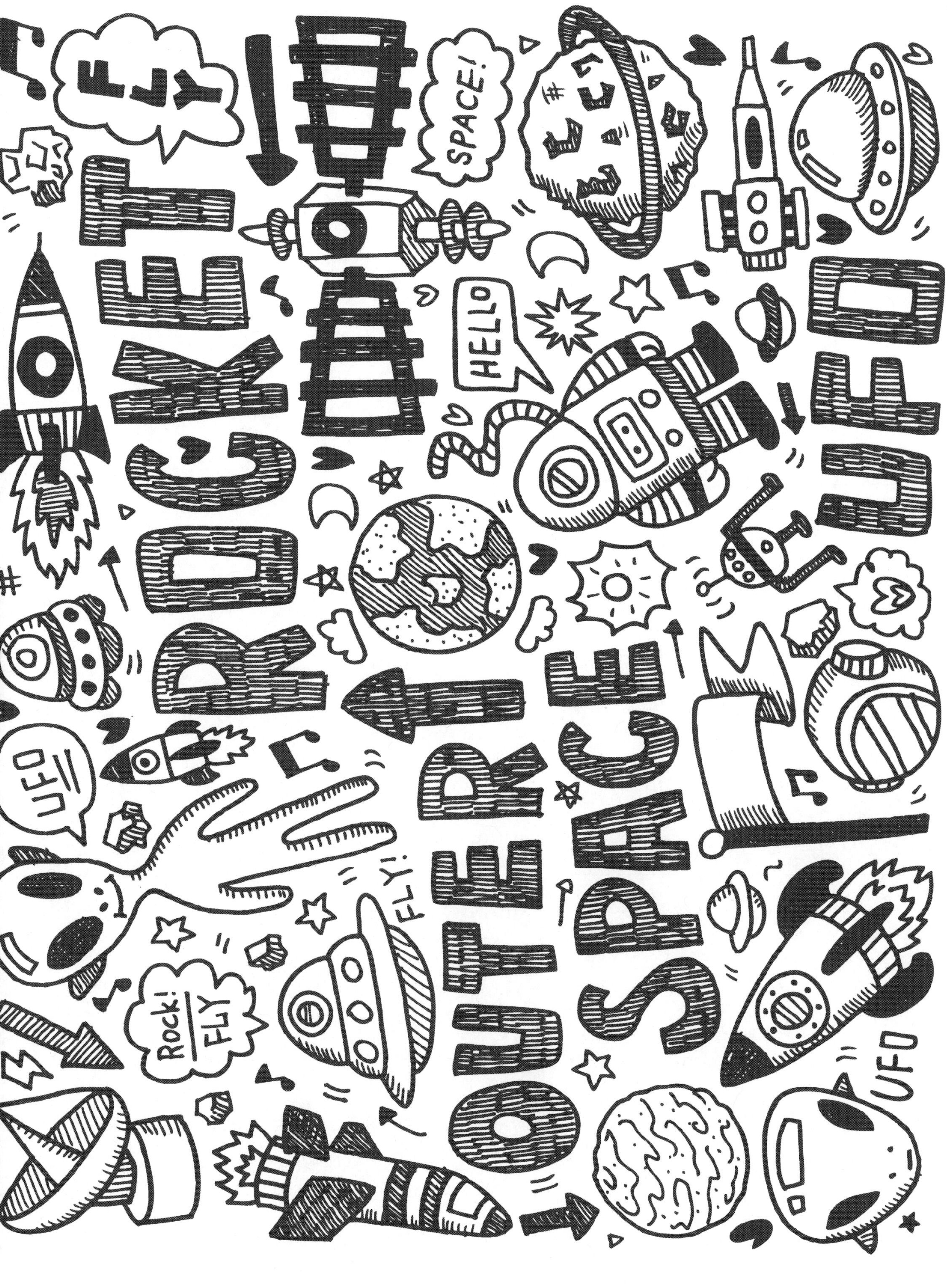
FLY
ROCKET
SPACE!
HELLO
UFO
UFO
OUTER SPACE
FLY!
Rock!
FLY
UFO

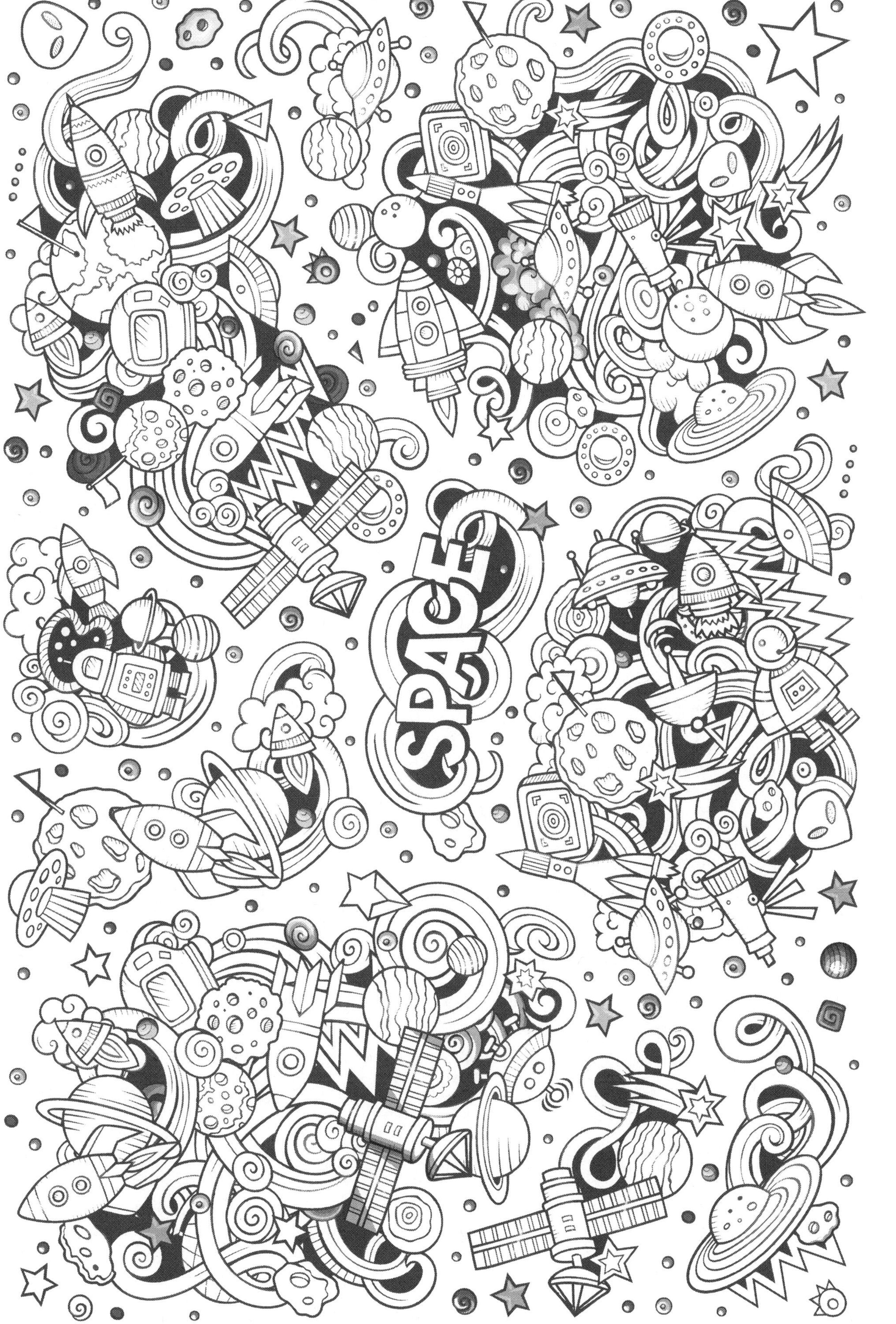
SPACE

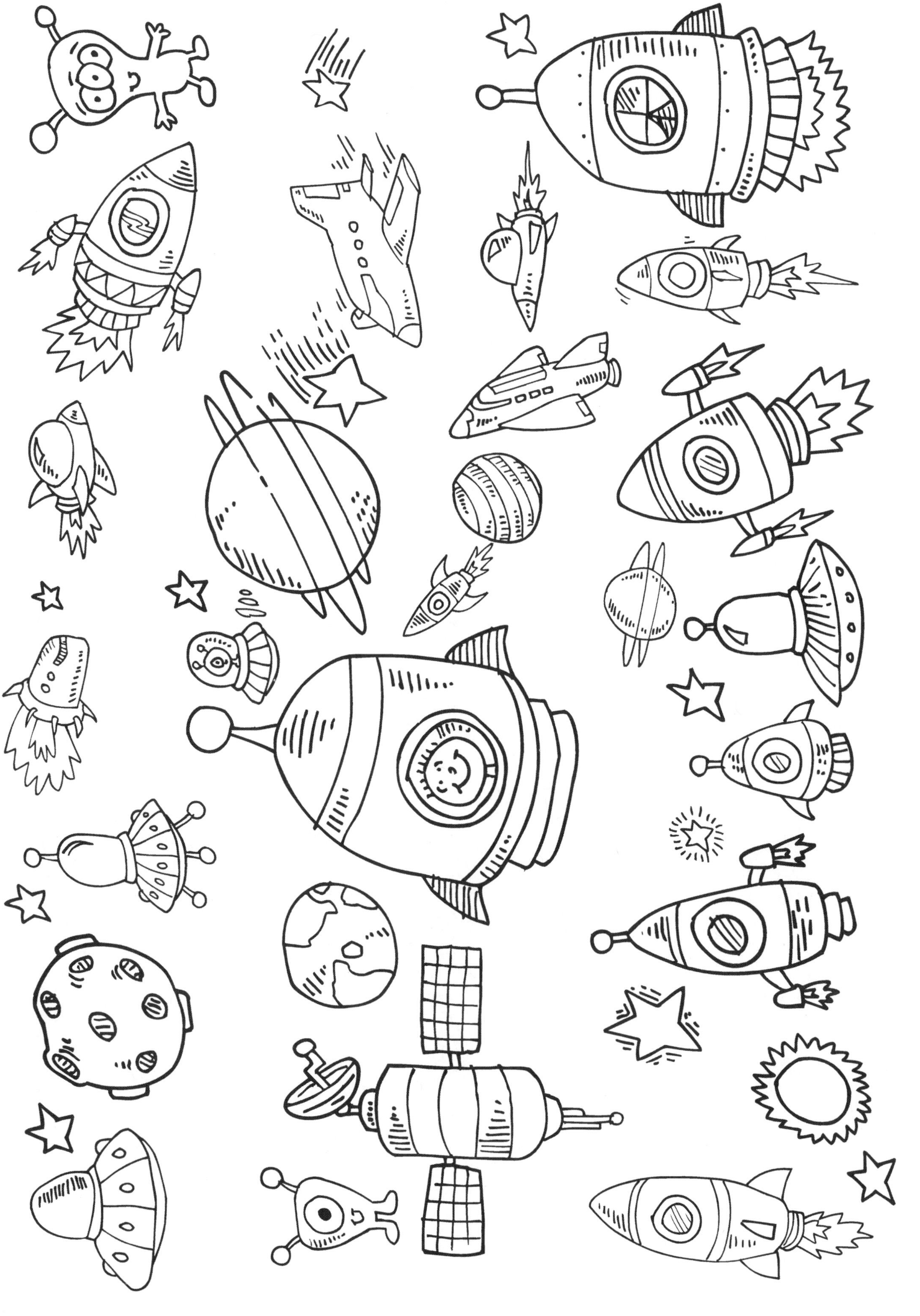

Made in the USA
Las Vegas, NV
04 December 2021

36098558R00050